BUILDING FAITH WITH THE BOOK OF MORMON

Glenn L. Pearson
Reid E. Bankhead

BUILDING FAITH WITH THE BOOK OF MORMON

Extensively enlarged and revised edition of the book *Teaching with the Book of Mormon*

To George F. Richards, Jr.
our beloved mission president
who introduced us to
the Book of Mormon as a missionary tool

Library of Congress Catalog Card Number: 86-71716

First Paperback Printing, 1992
Second Paperback Printing, 1995

Printed in the United States of America

Acknowledgments

We wish to express appreciation to Arden Roney, who, in May 1961, made a suggestion which led to the publication of this book's "great-grandfather." This caused us to crystallize our thinking concerning the manner in which we had gone about understanding and teaching the Book of Mormon for many years past.

We offer our heartfelt thanks to our wives, Ardith Hunsaker Pearson and Mary Smith Bankhead, who have kept us in the harness and have seen to it that the tugs were always tight.

Whatever good things of an academic nature we have done would not have happened if it had not been for the start given us at BYU by the late Dr. Sidney B. Sperry. He was the ideal administrator —a plain, loyal, kind man who offered brotherly encouragement along the path of righteousness and truth.

We thank all others who were responsible for our being at BYU and for our other positions of trust in which we were allowed the free exercise of our minds.

Introduction

"Jesus saith unto them, Have ye understood all these things? They say unto him, Yea, Lord.

"Then said he unto them, Therefore every scribe which is instructed into the kingdom of heaven is like unto a man that is an householder, which bringeth forth out of his treasure things new and old." (Matthew 13:51–52.)

The Book of Mormon is like such a scribe's treasure. It is full of "things new and old." All of its treasure is useful. Nothing which is said hereafter is intended to disparage or render ineffective any of the efforts of teachers or scholars who believe the Book of Mormon and teach or write about it. Every book has a main message and purpose, plus many "by-products" which may or may not have been suspected by the author. To some, Chaucer or Shakespeare may be more important as history than as literature or more important for linguistic research than for short-story plots. But, in their times, these authors had a purpose or a message that was more important to them than other considerations.

Our main purpose in writing this book is to help the reader begin to fill up his "bag" with treasures of knowledge out of the Book of Mormon that he can bring out whenever he is called upon to teach or preach. We say "begin" because the Book of Mormon is an almost infinite mine of spiritual treasure, and we will only scratch the surface and lay bare the mother lode.

We can look in the pages of the Book of Mormon for many things; but the best thing to look for is that which was intended for *us.* The authors of the book, first and foremost, desired to bring souls to Christ that they might be saved. It is not that we should ignore or refuse to take note of other things, but the book was written *to us* and *for us* as well as for the modern Lamanite and Jew. Should we fail to hear the somber warning of those who "whisper" to us "out of the dust" (2 Nephi 26:19), it will help us little to know on which side of the river Sidon the battle was fought when their life's blood was spilled.

Contents

Studying the Book of Mormon

Various Approaches

1. The Book of Mormon can be studied as literature. It is not representative of the best in Nephite literature according to Moroni (Mormon 9:32–33), but it contains some rather beautiful pieces of prose, poetry, and psalmody. At least, if we use the words *poetry* and *psalmody* in the broad and loose sense used by modern poets and Bible students, there are poems and psalms in the Book of Mormon. Rhyme, meter, and beat probably do not survive translation very well. What we have in our language may be but a shadow of the poetic forms and feelings that were there in the original.

2. Some remarkable and valuable inferences have been drawn from studies of evidences for the truth of the Book of Mormon that come from within the book. Consider as an example the proper nouns in the Book of Mormon. These certainly did not come from a fertile imagination. Where could Joseph Smith have obtained them? Why do they prove helpful in defending the Book of Mormon when investigated without prejudice? Dr. Hugh Nibley's two books, *Lehi in the Desert and The World of the Jaredites* and *An Approach to the Book of Mormon* are the classical works in this area. These contributions alone would have justified his having lived.

3. Akin to a study of such evidences is a study of discoveries in anthropology, archaeology, and geography that tend to corroborate the Book of Mormon story. Some very exciting artifacts have been collected and catalogued. To a converted "Mormon," the evidence seems too great to be passed off as coincidence.

4. Another approach to Book of Mormon study is the story approach. In this method, the student or teacher usually emphasizes the information that tells where the Book of Mormon people went and what they did. When such information is followed by a helpful lesson, this can be a very effective way to teach morals and ethics. Of course, similar lessons can be taught quite as effectively from the writings of the world's great poets and from great novels. We might also call this the anecdotal approach. With some, it is more historical; with others more moral. But it rarely gets close to the heart of things if storytelling is all that is done. On the other hand, all methods of studying and teaching the Book of Mormon will profit if allied with a knowledge of history of the Book of Mormon peoples. With all of our searchings and ponderings back and forth on specific doctrines, we should occasionally sit down and read the book from cover to cover as we would a novel.

5. Finally, we can study the book as that which it claims to be. The four preceding approaches to the Book of Mormon are all useful, all valid. A complete study of the book would have to include them. But the main message of the book could be neglected if no more were done with it than is generally implied in the above four approaches.

What the Book Claims to Be

The title page of the Book of Mormon states that its purpose is to convince both Jew and Gentile that Jesus is the Christ, and to reacquaint the Lamanites and other branches of the house of Israel with the promises made to their fathers and with the Lord's intention of keeping those promises. Elsewhere we learn that the Book of Mormon is a witness of the Bible. (Mormon 7:8–9; 2 Nephi 3:12; 29:3–14.) One of the clearest declarations of intent is found in these words of Nephi:

> And it mattereth not to me that I am particular to give a full account of all the things of my father, for they cannot be written upon these plates, for I desire the room that I may write of the things of God.
>
> For the fulness of mine intent is that I may persuade men to come unto the God of Abraham, and the God of Isaac, and the God of Jacob, and be saved.
>
> Wherefore, the things which are pleasing unto the world I do not write, but the things which are pleasing unto God and unto those who are not of the world.
>
> Wherefore, I shall give commandment unto my seed, that they shall not occupy these plates with things which are not of worth unto the children of men. (1 Nephi 6:3–6.)

Think how happy the world would have been to find the Book of Mormon plates, to grub them up with the archaeologist's shovel, and then (if they weren't melted down for their gold or declared a fraud deliberately planted to deceive them) to set the world's greatest linguists to work translating them! They could have had a heyday. They could have squabbled over the gold plates for at least a hundred years and never agreed on a thing. Of course, the book would then have had no value as scripture. It is precisely because the gold plates came the way they did and were then taken away that the Book of Mormon can be the "keystone of our religion"—its source as well as its message must be accepted on faith.

Or think how happy the world would be if the book's pages were filled with maps and other data which would prove its authenticity so that the need, as they might suppose, for exercising faith could be eliminated! Of course, that too is a snare and a delusion. But who has not secretly wished that the gates of a city could be found with the word *Zarahemla* inscribed in several languages across its top?

Instead it is such a book that those "who are not of this world" love it for the good that is in it and the good to which it bears witness. They need no external proof. It leads them to the God of Israel, Jesus Christ, and shows them how to be saved through him and his gospel. The Spirit bears witness to their souls. (Moroni 10:4–5; Alma 5:44–48; 2 Nephi 33:10–11; Doctrine and Covenants 50:13–21.)

In order for the Book of Mormon to realize its purpose of bringing souls to Christ in the latter days, it must do two things. One is that it must tell us about Christ and his gospel in a plain manner so that there can be no confusion. Great and wonderful as the Bible is, that book as we have it today does not do that, as is evidenced by the myriad interpretations that arise out of it.

But to tell of Christ and his gospel is not enough. The book also must fortify the reader against those ideas which exclude the gospel from his mind or prevent him from seeing it in its true light. Some beliefs are compatible and some are not. Love and mercy are compatible. Love and self-preservation (personal or national defense) are generally compatible. But love is not compatible with hate or aggression. Love cannot possess a mind that is full of hate and aggression. Love cannot conquer a nation which excludes love and freedom. So it is with many other ideas or states of mind and being in the world today. In his infinite foreknowledge, God so fashioned the Book of Mormon that it anticipated the needs of our times. It contains a warning against the evil philosophies and practices of our day.

Christ and His Gospel

The Book of Mormon message about Christ and his gospel can be divided into at least the following eight areas:

1. *His divinity.* This area includes the prophecies of his coming, announcements that he is the Son of God, explanations of his being an agent for the Father, and so on. In Mosiah 15, Abinadi gives four reasons why Jesus is rightly called the Father: (a) heirship or kinship,

(b) agency or proctorship, (c) as the Creator, and (d) as the Father of the faithful. In Ether 3, Christ's role in the Creation is made known. Many other passages declare his godhood.

2. *The legal necessity of a Redeemer.* The Book of Mormon clarifies the meaning and nature of sin, law, punishment, mercy, grace, and justice. It tells why obedience to law without a Redeemer would avail nothing. It gives the terms upon which mercy can claim the sinner without destroying justice. No one can know his need for a Redeemer without knowing these things well enough to cause him to put his trust only in Christ.

3. *The nature of the Atonement.* In King Benjamin's great sermon—and elsewhere in the Book of Mormon—we are brought to the realization that Jesus' atonement was an expiatory act by a divine being. His agony in Gethsemane for our sins caused him to bleed at every pore. As he hung from the cross—his heart broken, made to feel forsaken by his Father—he was offered as the last sacrifice, the spear of a heathen soldier doing service as the sacrificial knife. We are bought with his blood if we will plead for him to apply the price.

4. *The initiation of repentance by the broken heart and contrite spirit.* When Benjamin finished his sermon, he discovered that it had had a most profound effect upon his hearers. An even more pronounced change came over some others who had been more wicked. Alma the Younger and some Lamanite royalty were stricken as though dead. Zeezrom became exceedingly ill and would have died if God had not sent Alma to heal him. By these stories and in other ways, the Book of Mormon brings its readers to a realization of the enormity of sin and the necessity of recognizing our guilt.

5. *The first principles of the gospel.* A knowledge of the four foregoing areas is prerequisite to faith in Christ. But it must be an active faith—a "faith unto repentance." (Alma 34:15–17.) Nowhere is it possible to get a better understanding of the purpose and meaning of the first principles of the gospel than in the Book of Mormon.

6. *The rebirth.* Of course, the spiritual rebirth is embraced in the first four principles when they are properly taught and understood. But one should take some things apart and look at the separate pieces and then put them back together. The Book of Mormon does this with the principle or process of being born again, being born of the Spirit, or putting on Christ. Alma's description of his own experience, as retold in Alma 36, is beautiful and clear beyond comparison. One might have gone through the formality of baptism and the

laying on of hands; but if he has not received the new Spirit, his actions have been in vain. Among the Book of Mormon peoples, the second generation often apostatized. The lesson seems to be that, while a rebirth will produce certain works, the formality of pushing people into those same works will not necessarily produce a rebirth. That is where the broken heart and the contrite spirit come in.

7. *The need for enduring to the end.* Since much of the Book of Mormon is to or about those who are or were members of the Church, it is understandable that the doctrine of enduring to the end is contained in nearly every chapter in either an implicit or explicit form. The book is a great instrument to "succor the weak, lift up the hands which hang down, and strengthen the feeble knees." (Doctrine and Covenants 81:5; see also Galatians 6:1–4.)

8. *The moral life of a Saint.* As one might reasonably expect, Jesus repeated to the Nephites that greatest of sermons, which we commonly call the Sermon on the Mount. But many other choice sermons are given and many stories are told to guide the feet of a Saint in the path of righteousness. The reader is told the formula or guide which will determine right from wrong in any situation. In this study guide, this formula is called "the moral imperative." One explanation of it is found in Moroni 7.

Warning Against Modern Pitfalls

The first thing we must realize if we are to benefit by the warning voice of the Book of Mormon is that it was addressed to the people of our day. The words of those who have slumbered in the dust were tailored to fit our needs. Then they were hidden up and saved for our time.

> And no one need say they shall not come, for they surely shall, for the Lord hath spoken it; for out of the earth shall they come, by the hand of the Lord, and none can stay it; and it shall come in a day when it shall be said that miracles are done away; and it shall come even as if one should speak from the dead. (Mormon 8:26.)

> Hearken, O ye Gentiles, and hear the words of Jesus Christ, the Son of the living God, which he hath commanded me that I should speak concerning you, for, behold he commandeth me that I should write, saying:
>
> Turn, all ye Gentiles, from your wicked ways; and repent of your evil doings, of your lyings and deceivings, and of your whoredoms, and of

> your secret abominations, and your idolatries, and of your murders, and your priestcrafts, and your envyings, and your strifes, and from all your wickedness and abominations, and come unto me, and be baptized in my name, that ye may receive a remission of your sins, and be filled with the Holy Ghost, that ye may be numbered with my people who are of the house of Israel. (3 Nephi 30:1–2.)

Two-Way Warning

The Book of Mormon tells us stories about Korihor, Nehor, Sherem, Zeezrom, Alma the Younger, Corianton, Laman, and others whose faults or mistakes are just as common in our day as in times of old. They are a warning to us. These men were deceived by Satan. Korihor taught many things which are similar to the teachings of Karl Marx. Nehor was a great "liberal" in the same sense that the word is now appropriated by many who take what they call a liberal view of religion and politics. And they show the same intolerance for opposition that he showed. No Latter-day Saint need be deceived by any of the modern Sherems, Nehors, Korihors, and their like. We have been adequately warned. As students and teachers of the Book of Mormon, we ought to ponder the apostate prototypes in the Book of Mormon and try to see them in our modern culture. And this we will do if we always keep paramount the idea that we must study and teach the Book of Mormon as a warning voice to our day.

Studying the Warning Message

1. *The student of the Book of Mormon must first settle his mind about the truth of Joseph Smith's story.* He must have a testimony that this story is true; that is, he must accept it on faith or by the knowledge conferred by the Spirit. Any feeling that Joseph Smith's mind created the book rather than that it was translated from the gold plates damages the usefulness of the Book of Mormon. Furthermore, the student must not fall into the trap that some weak-faithed or confused members have fallen into; that is, he must not accept the book as a translation and then dismiss some of its teachings by saying that the Nephites just didn't know any better than to believe such common superstitions of their times. It is not man's right to dismiss or doubt

any teaching of the Book of Mormon. For instance, if the Book of Mormon confirms the fall of Adam, the Flood, the confusion of tongues at the time of the tower of Babel, and similar matters, these things must be accepted if the Book of Mormon is to be accepted as having come the way Joseph Smith said it came. Those who think otherwise simply are confused or do not have an adequate testimony and have not fully made up their minds to believe the Book of Mormon.

God has the power to tell people what he wants them to know and bring them to understanding (not misunderstanding) in their own tongue. (Doctrine and Covenants 1:24.) The voice of God told the Three Witnesses that the book was true and the translation correct. Joseph Smith said it was "the most correct of any book on earth, and the keystone of our religion, and a man would get nearer to God by abiding by its precepts, than by any other book." (Joseph Smith, *History of the Church,* 4:461; see also 3 Nephi 5:18; D&C 17:6; 20:6–10.)

If there is any error in the teachings of the Book of Mormon, no man, by human means, will be able to discover it. If Lehi said that Adam introduced sin and death into the world, it was so. Had he a knowledge of modern geology, paleontology, or biology, his story would have been no different. Anyone who accepts the book in any less degree than this fails to understand the potential power and influence of the book. What is even worse, he may have condemned his own soul or delayed the progress of those who listen to him if he teaches ideas which cast doubt on the truth of the Book of Mormon.

2. *The teacher or student must have a correct understanding of what is meant by the idea that the gospel embraces all truth.* This idea does not mean that the mind is a sponge and knowledge is water and it doesn't matter where the sponge soaks up water as long as it is soaking it up. When the Brethren have taught that the gospel embraces all truth, they did not mean that all knowledge is of equal value. They have clearly taught that some truths should hold a higher position on our hierarchies of value than other truths. We should seek spiritual knowledge earlier and more diligently than secular knowledge—even than secular knowledge that has been proven true by all necessary tests. The prophets have taught that we shouldn't believe everything the world believes. When Brigham Young, for instance, said that the gospel embraces all truth, he was using "gospel" to mean all of our religion. It is true that we claim our religion embraces all truth and is compatible with all truth. But we

are selective about what we accept as true. We screen the world's beliefs. And the first screen always should be the Book of Mormon.

We must not think of knowledge as though it were somewhat analogous to a spectrum, with the subjects ranging from accounting to zymurgy, let us say, with all subjects of equal value. Some seem to feel that, if the gospel embraces all truth, Shakespeare is as important as Moses; that salvation is an endless process of learning, and the more you learn, the more you realize that you know nothing. If one accepts the premises from which these people reason, he can only conclude that a lifetime spent on one segment of the knowledge spectrum is just as useful, just as much an indication of love for the gospel, as a lifetime spent on any other segment, and that is definitely not the case.

This philosophy must be eliminated if one is to teach or learn the best that is in the scriptures. There are, as Paul said, two areas of knowledge: that which can be learned by men and that which can be learned only with the help of revelation. (1 Corinthians 2:11.) The "things of God" can be known only by revelation. One must fully partake of the spirit of Jacob's words:

> Behold, great and marvelous are the works of the Lord. How unsearchable are the depths of the mysteries of him; and it is impossible that man should find out all his ways. And no man knoweth of his ways save it be revealed unto him; wherefore, brethren, despise not the revelations of God. (Jacob 4:8.)

In saying the above, of course, there is no intent to imply that, under the right set of priorities, the learning of man cannot be very productive and worthwhile. (2 Nephi 9:28–29, 42–43.)

3. *The student or teacher must get a correct understanding of the nature of man.* Man is not necessarily essentially good or utterly depraved. Some people are quite good, some quite evil. None are born with a load of guilt or blame; but, as they grow up, some prove to be very good and some become very depraved. But *all* are fallen. *All* are lost. Without the Redeemer, none can be saved.

We are not just the product of heredity and environment. While we do not bring with us to earth a *memory* of a premortal experience, we do bring the characters we formed in that previous life. We developed those characters over a comparatively long period of time—how long we do not know. But we know we are here to be tested, tried, and finally judged. God's judgment would be a farce if there weren't something eternal inside of us that we brought with us, for which we alone are responsible. We are free to improve or get worse. We can repent or we can refuse to repent. We cannot be coerced into goodness by God, because he has said he will not use coercion and he is a God of truth. But he can and will hold us accountable. He warns us and offers help all the day long; but when night comes, we must face the consequences of the preparations we have made in the day. We need to listen to what *God* says and not change it to fit our own prejudices.

4. *Teachers and students must learn to relate the Book of Mormon to their own times, not just the times of the ancient writers of the book.* They must not approach it with scholarly detachment, but must become involved in it. Then they will identify each character with their counterparts in our times. They will believe that the theology is true, will accept the moral code as their own way of life, and will identify the false religious and political philosophies of our day for what they are and thus be forewarned.

5. *Teachers and students should study the Book of Mormon itself.* While study guides have value, the greatest value comes from reading the Book of Mormon itself and then pondering and praying about its message. The better study guides tend to lead people into the Book of Mormon itself, while the less valuable study guides tend to lead them out of the Book of Mormon and into commentaries and other readings *about* the Book of Mormon. You cannot get the same witness of the Spirit concerning the Book of Mormon by studying everything except the Book of Mormon that you can by studying the book itself.

Paying the Price for Knowledge

It takes time and hard work to learn anything worth learning. The time spent must be active, effective, dedicated, productive time. There must be practice, repetition, and participation of some sort. It usually takes an hour a day for eight to ten years to produce a somewhat accomplished piano player. Athletes practice long hours for years and give a sport their best all-out effort. Such learners never really know whether it is all going to pay until the scholarship or the contract is offered to them.

In the so-called exact sciences—mathematics, physics, chemistry—and in the applied sciences, such as engineering and medicine, students are expected to attend lecture courses besides reading large and detailed texts. Then they are required to go into laboratories and do tests and exercises which illustrate the things they have read and heard. In addition, they have problems to work at home that must be done in writing. Courses in grammar demand a great deal of written work in class and at home. Students must learn to diagram sentences, to write proper essays, themes, and term papers.

All important areas of learning are difficult and require a great deal of "homework." Students generally know that and usually are willing to pay the price. Yet, none of the rewards for any of these academic, athletic, or artistic efforts are as important as the rewards for learning the knowledge offered in the scriptures. Should we expect it to be easier to provide for our spiritual welfare than for our temporal welfare?

In one of the great sermons recorded in the Book of Mormon, Jacob decried the materialism and adultery of the Nephites. With reference to their materialism, he said this:

> Think of your brethren like unto yourselves, and be familiar with all and free with your substance, that they may be rich like unto you.
>
> But before ye seek for riches, seek ye for the kingdom of God.
>
> And after ye have obtained a hope in Christ ye shall obtain riches, if ye seek them; and ye will seek them for the intent to do good—to clothe the naked, and to feed the hungry, and to liberate the captive, and administer relief to the sick and the afflicted. (Jacob 2:17–19.)

What Jacob is saying is that the first quest is a search for the kingdom (the true Church) and for a hope in Christ (the assurance of salvation given by the First Comforter, or gift of the Holy Ghost). No earthly goals should preempt this great quest. Yet most members put worldly success ahead of gaining a testimony of the truth of the Book of Mormon and all that goes with it. They promise themselves they will get around to it after they graduate, or after they are settled in their careers. By and by it becomes "when the family is raised." And so on. Most members finally die without having even read the entire standard works through once. Yet they have promised themselves a thousand times to get it done. If the whole Book of Mormon had been read as often as the first three chapters of 1 Nephi, we would be a Church of, perhaps, a hundred times the influence we presently are. We even may have removed the curse God put on us for neglecting the Book of Mormon. (See D&C 84:54–58.)

The authors would like to suggest that all would profit by recording their thoughts about the scriptures in written form. We are never too old to start doing "homework." Everyone tends to collect the best that comes "across his desk." You will find that, if you try to write your own thoughts, by and by these scraps of paper or journal notes will become some of your most prized possessions. With such an important and eternal subject as the fulness of the gospel presented in the Book of Mormon, how could you expect or hope to learn it without producing your very best effort in written homework? The Lord has said we must "awake and arouse [our] faculties." (Alma 32:27.) We are told to seek "with real intent." (Moroni 10:4.) And we are often reminded that "faith without works is dead." (James 2:21.)

One form your "homework" might take is writing dialogues. Hundreds of students have found this a very useful method of preparing for missionary work in the mission field or with neighbors at home. What you do is take a particular doctrine you have learned and imagine yourself teaching it to someone else. Give him or her a name and then write a dialogue between that person and yourself. Try to anticipate what the responses and objections will be and how you will meet them. If you can pick a specific individual you already know, you will find it easier to predict his or her reactions. By and by you will have a system worked out that will produce success in your missionary endeavors. It also will result in spiritual experiences that will bring joy equal to anything you ever have experienced.

Another form your writing might take is that of making lists of ideas and concepts on each subject you study. Read, study, and ponder the passages suggested in this book or in the Topical Guide (TG) which is found in the latest edition of the Bible published by the Church. Then sit down and try to make a list of concepts on that subject. For instance, on baptism, you might include in your list these concepts or ideas: (1) Baptism is a covenant. (2) Baptism is the door or gate through which we must enter to get onto the path that leads to eternal life. (3) Baptism places us under covenant to keep all the covenants that have been accepted by common consent. (4) Baptism obligates us to mourn with those who mourn, comfort those who stand in need of comfort, and so forth. (See Mosiah 18:8–10.) (5) Baptism has no value without faith in Christ and repentance. (6) Baptism is invalid if we do not forgive our enemies and all who have harmed us. (7) And so on.

As you write these lists, try to bring the Book of Mormon into your life today. The present Church manuals call this "likening the scriptures unto us." This idea is derived from 1 Nephi 19:23. It is an antidote to the "me-here-and-now" attitude of many selfish humanistic movements of the sixties, seventies, and eighties.

Ask yourself, "What is this passage trying to tell me about my life, my friends, my family, my school work, my government, my neighbor, my mission, my Church activity. What is it trying to tell me about 'the great plan of the Eternal God' (Alma 34:9), about my Lord and Savior Jesus Christ, about my eternal life?"

When something comes to your mind from the message of the scriptures, combine the language of holy writ and your own language and express the idea or concept in writing. Make a numbered list in writing of these ideas and concepts as you read the scriptures on various subjects. This is your homework assignment. Those who have done this testify that it bears good fruit. It is worth the effort, determination, and work that it requires.

The following list is a recapitulation and expansion of the reasons why you should do this written homework:

1. It is your opportunity to express yourself in "Book of Mormon language" as you learn to understand it and adopt it as your own. A "Book of Mormon man or woman" is recognized by his or her speech patterns and ideas about every facet of life. If he speaks the language, you know he has been there.

2. The lists give you an opportunity to see what you have learned from studying the scriptures. It is said that you don't know anything until you can teach it and that writing makes your thinking more accurate. If you put it in a sentence or a paragraph, you begin to look at it and wonder if it will pass inspection. This makes you more careful about what you say.

3. These lists or writing exercises give you an opportunity to see how well you can form thoughts in your mind and then express them in writing for your own or someone else's reading. Only practice can make you a writer. Writing is among the hardest work there is; but that is no more of an excuse to stop trying than it would be to stop trying to improve your percentage at throwing the basketball through the hoop. All good things come hard.

4. Your writing will serve as a complete set of notes for later use. And these notes will be a by-product of your study of the Book of Mormon. They will be a reminder of the ground you have been over.

5. This "homework" can be a future reference and outline for you as you make and accept teaching assignments in your life as a parent and as a servant of the Lord in his Church.

If you often review and revise what you have written, you will find that a lot of your homework for future assignments was completed when you first began to earnestly study the Book of Mormon and the other scriptures.

One other thing on this written work: Except for assignments from teachers, who assign homework for their own specific purposes, develop your own system and organization of writing. We generally are more productive when we are being creative instead of just imitating someone else.

How This Book Is Organized

The main body of this book is made up of separate sections or topics, such as baptism, faith, repentance, and so on. In turn, each topic has five parts: (1) a title, including an acronym or code name which serves as a short title; (2) an explanation of the content of the topic; (3) a "take-off passage"; (4) a list of scriptural references called "other passages"; and (5) a set of "study questions." Following is a detailed explanation of the purpose and content of each of these five parts:

1. *The title and acronym* identify the subject matter in the section or topic. If you find the title unclear or inadequate, just read the first few sentences of the explanatory section.

The acronym or code name (e.g., B for Baptism), which is set off by bullets to the right of the title, serves additional purposes. Like all acronyms, it serves as a short title. This makes it possible to refer back and forth in this book from one section to another more conveniently. And it is the basis of a marking system which is illustrated in the appendix. If you follow this marking system, you may find it desirable to subdivide some of the acronyms—like B1, B2, B3, and so forth. This will make it possible for you to separate the passages on that subject into appropriate subtopics.

2. *The explanatory section* has the purpose of giving unity and direction to the set of references which follow it. It is not meant as a full explanation of the subject under investigation, but as a means of indicating what you might look for as you study the passages listed. Of course, you may find things you value more highly than any we have mentioned. That is one of the things we hope will happen.

3. *The Take-off Passage* serves several purposes. One purpose is to serve as the starting place for your marking system if you decide to use ours or one of your own. If you use the acronyms we have suggested, or a set you have made up yourself, you can write this acronym in the margin where the take-off passage appears in your Book of Mormon. Don't feel compelled to use our take-off passage. You should start with the passage you feel is the best starting place. Then you can write another passage in the margin of your Book of Mormon by that one. This other passage should be the next one you want to go to on the subject suggested by the acronym.

You will note that our take-off passage for Baptism (B) was Mosiah 18:8–18. (That was President Harold B. Lee's favorite passage on the subject of baptism.) The next passage we give is 2 Nephi 31:5–17, which tells why Jesus had to be baptized and why we have to be baptized. The next passage is 3 Nephi 11:21–28, the one in which Jesus himself tells us how baptism is to be done. The next passage is Moroni 8, which absolutely forbids infant baptism and gives a highly theological treatise on baptism and the doctrines immediately related to it.

You may wish to write "B" in the margin by each one of the above scriptures. And you may wish to write all of the references listed in the Baptism (B) section by every other passage listed. (See sample page in Appendix.) Or you may wish to list just one passage by each other passage. In any event, all this is just by way of suggestion for a system by which you can have a whole series of ready-made sermons or lessons outlined in the margins of your scriptures. If you are called out of the congregation to speak, all you have to do is thumb through your scriptures until you see an acronym that you feel prompted to start following back and forth. Then you can speak "as one having authority, and not as the scribes and Pharisees."

Some have listed all the acronyms, together with their take-off passages, in the front of their copies of the Book of Mormon. Then all they have to do when called upon for a speech or lesson is to prayerfully go over the list until they feel inspired in the selection of a topic. Of course, the idea is not to just read out the passages in turn—though that would be better than many could do without such an aid. The idea is to read each passage in turn and then explain to your audience how it clarifies the topic upon which you are speaking.

4. *The Other Passages* section is just what the name and the information in section 3, above, imply. If you decide to use the acronyms as a marking system, do not get in too big a hurry to cross-reference all of the "other passages" to each other, especially if there are a lot of them. Cross-reference them as they become fully meaningful to you. Also, consult the Topical Guide for additional passages. Be sure you understand the connection of one passage to another. Avoid too many that are simply repetitive. Think in terms of a logical flow for a sermon, and reference them accordingly.

Another way to approach this marking system is to combine it with the Topical Guide (TG) in the new edition of the scriptures. In that case, you may wish to circle or underline footnotes in the TG and in the Book of Mormon/Triple Combination index, and at the bottom of the page and write the acronym you wish to use in a prominent place on the page in such a manner that, when you see this acronym and the circled footnotes, you will remember why you did it. If you master the TG and sprinkle acronyms in appropriate places in your scriptures, you will soon find that you have developed the ability to discourse on almost any subject that can properly come up in your Church assignments.

5. *The Study Questions* section is meant to stimulate thought and analysis about the particular subject being studied. These questions are framed on the assumption that the reader has looked up the passages and pondered them. Still, it is suggested that the questions be read once before the "other passages" are read. That will help the reader find further implications in these passages. Then he can go back to the questions and give them a second try.

The authors do not claim to have presented all the passages on any given subject, or even a significant portion in some cases. You may find what you consider better passages when you start searching on your own initiative or through the TG. Also, this is by no means an exhaustive list of Book of Mormon subjects or concepts. It is an illustration of a system of studying and can be used as a system for marking the scriptures. We have tried to use what have been to us the most useful passages. We have also presented some useful and less often observed subject areas.

You will note that some sections have many references and some have only a few. One reason for that is that one needs only a few passages on some subjects to give one plenty to study or talk about. In other cases, even though the material is lengthy, there are so many ramifications that it is necessary to show some of them, and the only way that can be done is by listing a lot of passages. In some large areas such as repentance, for instance, we have used what almost might be called a random selection. You may want to subdivide these sections and add many references.

You will also discover that there is considerable overlapping on some subjects. This is inevitable because there are many different issues raised within a single verse of some of the best Book of Mormon sermons. Study the passages first, and then decide which passages to use in your marking system. Perhaps it might be well to use an inexpensive copy of the Book of Mormon the first time you try a marking system. You will not regret the practice.

The passages we have used are mainly expository in nature. That is, we have selected passages with an emphasis on doctrine. Next you may want to find good anecdotal passages to add interest to your lessons and sermons. For example, the great prayer recorded in John 17 is illustrative of the principle of prayer, while the prayer of the

Lamanite king in Alma 22 can be used in a story approach to prayer. Of course, any theological or expository passage can be introduced by telling the story in the context.

In the following pages the subjects are arranged chronologically by take-off passage. That is, they come in the order the take-off passages appear in the text of the Book of Mormon. An alphabetic index to these subjects, based on the acronyms, appears at the end of the book.

We hope this will be only the beginning of your systematic study of the scriptures. If you will pay the price, you can find great treasures of knowledge in the scriptures:

> And again, the elders, priests and teachers of this church shall teach the principles of my gospel, which are in the Bible and the Book of Mormon, in the which is the fulness of the gospel.
>
> And they shall observe the covenants and church articles to do them, and these shall be their teachings, as they shall be directed by the Spirit.
>
> And the Spirit shall be given unto you by the prayer of faith; and if ye receive not the Spirit ye shall not teach. (D&C 42:12–14.)

Study Topics

The Promises to Israel Are to Be Fulfilled • PI •

The title page of the Book of Mormon tells us that one of the Lord's purposes, in preparing and producing the book, was to remind the house of Israel that it was not cast off forever and that he would fulfill all his promises to Israel. That is quite significant, considering that most of the world thinks of the Jews as the only Israelites. Indeed, the Jews have wrongly appropriated the name *Israel* for their homeland. It would have been more accurate to call it *Judah.* That was the name of their nation in antiquity. Israel was the name of the nation of the ten tribes which were later lost in the "north countries."

But, then, we must go even further than that. For instance, the Northern Europeans and many others may have more of the blood of Israel than either the Jews or the American Indians. Doctrine and Covenants 86:9 tells us that we Latter-day Saints are the "lawful heirs [of the keys of the priesthood, which is Joseph's birthright], according to the flesh, and have been hid from the world with Christ in God." The fifth chapter of Jacob tells all about this intermingling of the branches of Israel with the rest of the world. And Jeremiah foresaw that the ten lost tribes of Israel were in the same "north countries" as the Jews. He saw them coming "together [with Judah] out of the land of the north to the land that I have given for an inheritance unto your fathers" in the last days. (Jeremiah 3:18.)

And we must go even further than that, for the Lord has declared by the voice of his prophets that the blood of Israel is now in all nations; and, as the Book of Mormon also promises, "black and white, bond and free, male and female" are all granted the full salvation of the Lord. (2 Nephi 26:33.) Abraham was promised that through his descendants all nations would have the blessings of the priesthood.

God made three general promises to Abraham, Isaac, and Jacob (Israel). These promises were (1) a numberless posterity, (2) a chosen land, and (3) the blessing of all nations through their posterity and the priesthood of their posterity. Later, other special promises were given. The first of these was to Joseph, the son of Jacob (Israel). He was promised a special, separate land and a righteous branch to be separated from the rest of the house of Israel. Later promises or assurances were given through Moses and other prophets that, even though all Israel should be scattered and many of them persecuted, the earlier promises would not be forgotten and there would be a day of restoration and gathering in which all the tribes of Israel would be united in peace under a King of kings and a Lord of lords. The Book of Mormon is a witness to the truth of these promises, and it is an assurance that none of them will be left unfulfilled.

Take-off Passage

Title Page (middle of second paragraph).

Other Passages

1 Nephi 15:12–18; 19:13–24; 22:9–12; 2 Nephi 3; 6:10–15; 9:1–3; 10:7–9; 25:15–18; 30:2–9; Alma 46:23–27; 3 Nephi 5:21–26; 15:8; 16:5; 20:12–46; 21; 29; Mormon 5:14; Ether 4:14, 15; Genesis 12:1–3; 48:8–22; 49; Deuteronomy 4:25–31; 33; 1 Chronicles 5:1, 2; Jeremiah 31:9, 18–20, 31–34; Hebrews 7:11–14; Abraham 2:8–11; Doctrine and Covenants 86:8–11.

Study Questions

1. What statements in the Book of Mormon clarify the blessing that Jacob gave Joseph in Genesis 49:22–26?
2. What do Latter-day Saints, American Indians, and Jews have in common right now? What more will they have in common in the future?
3. As the Lord fulfills his promises to all the tribes of Israel, how will it become more and more apparent that it is wrong to teach that there will be no revelation besides the Bible? How does this show that Revelation 22:18–21 has been misinterpreted by those who oppose modern revelation?
4. How can you use your knowledge of the nation of Joseph to get people interested in reading the Book of Mormon?
5. Which verses in the passages cited above show that Joseph's tribes (Ephraim and Manasseh) were to have (a) a separate and wealthy land, (b) a righteous branch broken off, (c) a very numerous posterity, (d) the keys of the gathering, (e) the keys of the Melchizedek Priesthood, and (f) additional revelation besides the Bible?

The Book of Mormon Was Written to Convince Both Jews and Gentiles That Jesus Is the Christ • JG •

In its present nuance, the word *Jew* refers to someone who affiliates with the Jewish religion or is known to be of Jewish lineage. A Gentile is someone who is not of Jewish lineage or religion. But it is not as simple as that. We really need to know what Lehi and his descendants meant by Jew and Gentile.

At the death of Solomon in the tenth century B.C., Israel split into two kingdoms: Israel and Judah. At the time Lehi and company left Jerusalem, most of the kingdom of Israel (also sometimes called Ephraim, Kingdom of the North, the Ten Tribes, and so on) had been carried away captive into parts of what is now Turkey, Syria, Iraq, Iran, and Afghanistan. A large number of them, possibly the majority, had escaped from that area into "the north countries." Some of them were still in Samaria, their homeland. Certain members of the tribes of Ephraim and Manasseh had left their tribal lands and joined the southern kingdom, Judah. Lehi and Ishmael came from this loyalist group. Since the tribe of Levi was always spread throughout all Israel, much of Levi was in the south. Also, when the Ten Tribes became idolatrous, many of the Levites migrated into the south lands. So in Lehi's day (600 B.C.) the following ten tribes were lost: Reuben, part of Levi, Zebulon, Issachar, Dan, Gad, Asher, Naphtali, Ephraim, and Manasseh. The prophets referred to them as Israel. But the reader of the Bible has to be careful, because the word *Israel* sometimes means all of Jacob's descendants and sometimes only Jacob himself. The context has to be read carefully.

The tribes that were left in the kingdom of Judah were Judah, Simeon (which tribe had no separate identity because that tribe had been lost in Judah), Benjamin, and part of Levi. Also there were those small parts of the tribes of Joseph. The ten tribes are counted as ten because of the part of Levi that was with them. And the three tribes of the south are only three because Simeon was included in Judah and not counted. That part of Ephraim and Manasseh were too few to count. Indeed, a careful reading of the Old Testament reveals that the kingdom of Judah probably included a small number from every tribe. It's likely that a very small number from the tribes of Judah, Simeon, and Benjamin, besides that large part of Levi, had ended up with the ten northern tribes. The division was not as cut and dried as some have made it out to be. The common folk among all the tribes didn't take the division as seriously as did the royalists among the tribes of Judah, Benjamin, and Ephraim. These common folk intermarried as they pleased and went where they pleased most of the time.

When Lehi and his descendants said "Jew," they meant anyone who was a citizen of the country of Judah. On that basis they still called themselves Jews. (See 2 Nephi 33:8.) Anyone else was a Gentile, that is, a foreigner. Theoretically they did not include the ten lost tribes as Gentiles. Yet in a practical sense they must have. For Joseph Smith is identified in the Book of Mormon both as a Gentile and as a descendant of Joseph. And it would be natural for them to think of the ten tribes as Gentiles, since those tribes had been lost among the nations. Actually the basic meaning of *gentile* is "the nations."

Gentile is a transliteration of a Hebrew word that means "nation" in its singular form or "nations" in its plural form. It also does service as the word for *alien, foreigner, stranger,* and so forth. Thus, before the kingdom split there were Israelites and "the nations," meaning outsiders. After the split and the loss of the ten tribes, there were Jews and "the nations," or Gentiles. Besides that, in the Hebrew Bible you will find that same word used by the writers to refer to the "nations" of Israel—the twelve tribes, or thirteen when you count Joseph as two. The translators, of course, took care of that for you by the various English translation words they used when they came across that Hebrew word.

We have to go one step further to grasp the full range of meanings in the word *gentile.* Paul, in Ephesians, set up a word play that uses the Gentile-versus-Jew idea to emphasize the power that conversion has to make us citizens of Christ's kingdom. He indicates that, after rebirth, the Jews and Gentiles were "no more strangers and foreigners, but fellowcitizens with the saints." (Ephesians 2:19.) In this sense the Church of Jesus Christ of any dispensation is the "homeland," or Israel, and all others are Gentiles, or aliens. In the LDS church, we tend to include ourselves, the Jews, the American Indians, and some of the Pacific Island peoples on the non-gentile side and all others on the gentile side.

It is not strange to find that one of the avowed purposes of the Book of Mormon is to convince the Jews that Jesus is the Christ; for those whom we know as Jews never accepted him. The Jews of Jesus' day who did accept him are now lost among the Gentiles. It also is not strange that the Book of Mormon was written to convince the Lamanites that Jesus is the Christ; for they do not know him by that name in their traditions. But it was strange in 1830 for a backwoods gentile boy (who didn't know he was an Israelite) to announce that the Book of Mormon was going to convince the *Gentiles* of Christ's divinity. In that day the Gentiles believed the Bible quite generally and hence claimed to believe in the divinity of Christ. Certainly Joseph Smith on his own never would have thought that the Gentiles he knew needed to be convinced that Jesus was the Christ. But they needed more convincing than he would have thought, and they need even more convincing now. Comparatively few in the Western world today believe in a Christ who continues to be a resurrected being. Therefore they reject him in anything approaching a Book of Mormon sense, which is the same sense as the New Testament. Indeed, most Americans and Europeans have become humanists since Joseph Smith's day. Even those who claim to be Christians are frequently more humanistic than Christian in the biblical sense. That is, they accept Darwin and Sagan over Moses on creation, and the "higher critics" over Paul and John on the reality and permanence of Jesus' resurrection. (For a definition of humanism, see H.)

Take-off Passage

Title Page (end of second paragraph).

Other Passages

1 Nephi 6:4; 2 Nephi 25:11–30; 26:12; 29:1–3; 33:10; 3 Nephi 29:8, 9; 30; Mormon 5:14–21; 8:35; Ether 12:41; Moroni 7:35; 10:30; Doctrine and Covenants 3:16–20.

Study Questions

1. Why would Latter-day Saints consider all members of other Christian churches to be Gentiles?

2. From a Book of Mormon point of view, why would other Christians, even their devout leaders and evangelists, have to be converted to Christ?

3. What does Nephi give as the real test of whether someone believes in Christ?

4. Who are the keepers of the gate and what must be done to enter into the path?

The Faults of Men Which the Book of Mormon Says It Might Contain Are Not Doctrinal Errors • FM •

Some have used the passages cited below as evidence that the Book of Mormon contains doctrinal errors and is unreliable as an absolute authority. Some of these people think Joseph Smith wrote the book. Others think the ancient Nephites wrote it, but that it contains the errors and superstitions of their less enlightened times. They believe, therefore, that the Book of Mormon and all other scriptures have to be submitted to their test of reason. In other words, whatever does not agree with the learned or scientific consensus of our day must be rejected as false. They believe, for instance, that while Lehi would have logically believed that Moses was right about the Creation and the fall of Adam, now that we have discovered evolution we know better. Therefore they think we should reject anything the Book of Mormon prophets wrote that disagrees with the modern view of man and creation.

A careful scrutiny of the passages listed in this section, however, will show that the writers were referring to their own human foibles that they had recorded, and to their grammar. These were the "mistakes of men" they mentioned. They were not referring to their theology. They made no apology for the doctrines they taught. Also, we have the word of God in the testimony of the Three Witnesses that the book is true. In section 1 of the Doctrine and Covenants the Lord says that he uses our own language for the purpose of bringing us to understanding, *not* misunderstanding. We can be sure that if there are doctrinal or historical errors in the Book of Mormon no human will ever discover them. Though all the world believe otherwise, if Lehi said the earth and everything in it was immortal until the Fall, it was so.

Take-off Passage

Title Page (last sentence).

Other Passages

Testimony of Three Witnesses; Mormon 8:12–17; 9:31–34; Ether 12:23–28, 35; Doctrine and Covenants 1:17–29; 17:5, 6; 18:1–5; 20:6–15; 68:4; 1 Corinthians 2:14.

Study Questions

1. Since none of our prophets have pointed out errors in Book of Mormon history and theology, how should we approach the "faults of men" statements in the book?
2. What limitations do men and women have that make it impossible for them to successfully criticize or explain away revelation?
3. How do you know that any attempt to discredit the Book of Mormon is destructive of faith and is inspired of the devil?

The Witnesses of the Book of Mormon Satisfy God's Laws Concerning Witnesses

• WBM •

Many express the opinion that the story about the gold plates being returned to the angel Moroni is a "convenient" escape from an embarrassing predicament. The faithful, however, can see that the story is just what should have been expected for the following reasons:

1. The same complaint could be made against the biblical account of the Resurrection—only chosen witnesses testified that Christ was risen. (Acts 10:39–41.)
2. Had the angel allowed the Church to keep the gold plates, the world would have found some reason to take them from us, or some thief would have stolen them.
3. If the world—or the Church—had the plates, the whole story could be treated as an archaeological discovery. The element of the supernatural would be gone. Without it, Joseph Smith's story could be treated in any number of ways different from the manner in which it must now be treated. Now it is either the truth or a hoax. If the plates were available (assuming they would have escaped being melted down by frontier rowdies), it could be said that Joseph Smith found them or that he made them. They could say that he found

some treasure, melted it down, beat it into sheets, and stamped nonsense characters on it. Or it could be said that his translation was not correct. The "experts" would probably say, "We don't know what it should be, since no scholar can translate it anyway. But we are sure Joseph Smith couldn't if the linguists cannot." And even if they did finally crack the "reformed Egyptian" and did translate it into the same words as Joseph Smith did, they would not have to treat it as revelation in any sense greater than they presently treat the Bible—which is essentially as the superstitious traditions of an ancient, ignorant people.

4. If it were possible that the gold plates could prove Joseph Smith's story, the last thing the Lord would do would be to let anyone but chosen witnesses see them. Giving everyone proof and eliminating the need for faith would destroy the very purpose of this life. Proving the Book of Mormon true is tantamount to proving the truth of the resurrection of Christ, the truth of the restoration of the gospel, and so forth. The Lord expects us to exercise faith first and get the proof "after the trial of your faith." (Ether 12:6.)

The practical value of this section (WBM) is that it forges one more link in the chain of the doctrine of witnesses. This is the doctrine which defines the Lord's method of testifying to the truth. One day the sinner will find himself wrapped around and bound up by this chain of the testimonies of witnesses sent by God to tell and substantiate his word and will. The sinner's condemnation will be that all he had to do was exercise his faith and he would have been justified.

Take-off Passage

The testimonies of the Three Witnesses and of the Eight Witnesses.

Other Passages

2 Nephi 11:3; 27:12–14; Ether 5:1–4; Deuteronomy 19:15–17; Luke 24:48; Acts 3:15; 4:33; 5:32; 10:39–41; 2 Corinthians 13:1; 2 Peter 1:16; Doctrine and Covenants 5:23–35; 17; 20:6–17. (See EWC.)

Study Questions

1. What are some significant differences between the testimony of the Three Witnesses and that of the Eight Witnesses?

2. What burden of proof is placed upon the reader of the Book of Mormon by the testimonies of the three and the eight?
3. Since none of the eleven witnesses denied his testimony, why cannot one successfully impeach it now?
4. When, or in what ways, are the readers of the Book of Mormon—not the Book of Mormon itself—on trial as they read and accept or reject it?
5. How could you use this section in missionary work?

We Must Have Determination in Grappling with Problems • DIG •

Even when our Heavenly Father gives us a commandment, he does not necessarily make it easy for us to comply with it. We sometimes have to surmount great obstacles to fulfill the commandments of the Lord. Joseph Smith's life is a testimony of this fact. The story of Nephi obtaining the brass plates is another example of this principle. Everyone who has struggled with the Lord for an answer to his prayers to the point where he has received the answer knows that it usually *does* consist of an all-out struggle. It is like Jacob's all-night wrestle with the Lord that left him crippled, or like the prayer of Enos that lasted all day and into the night.

One reason why we have to live by faith in this life is that we are forced to make decisions based on what we believe is right. We then have to follow through on those decisions—even if the way is hard. Making decisions and sticking with them, even when the going gets rough, is what develops or proves character. Even gaining the knowledge we need to be saved is a struggle. No one can do it for us. It comes "line upon line," and it has to be searched for and yearned for.

Take-off Passage

1 Nephi 3:7.

Other Passages

2 Nephi 4:15–35; Jacob 7:26; Enos; Mosiah 26:14; Alma 5:45, 46; 8:10–27; 17:2–5; 1 Thessalonians 1:5, 6; Doctrine and Covenants 58:1–7; 121:1–9. (For anecdotal material consider the story of the translation of the plates, or any of the many stories of Joseph

Smith's determination to serve the Lord in the face of opposition. Heber J. Grant's life was largely inspired by 1 Nephi 3:7. He overcame many things because of the inspiration he got from Nephi.)

Study Questions

1. What do you learn from Nephi's experience in building a ship, about our ability to receive help beyond our inherent abilities and environment?
2. How did Nephi benefit in having to struggle to obtain the brass plates and build the ship?
3. Do you believe a righteous government would save people from the opportunity to handle their own problems, to make mistakes and correct them, to fail and succeed, or to struggle to provide their own daily bread and nest egg for the future?
4. Do you believe you should vote for politicians who propose welfare legislation that would prevent you from learning self-reliance, faith in God, and courage?
5. Do you see any similarities between the welfare states now existing in many lands and the one Satan planned for us? (Moses 4:1.)
6. Why did God reject Satan's plan?
7. Why would God *not* answer your prayers about many things if you were an indecisive person who had not first tried to decide on a worthwhile or righteous course of action?

Does History Unfold by Chance or by Design? • HCD •

The Latter-day Saints worship a God who is omniscient and omnipotent; and they believe that he intervenes in the affairs of men in such a manner as to bring about his purposes without interfering with our right to be saved or damned as we choose. That is, no individual's free agency is interfered with, and yet the Lord can plan history in advance by where and when he places certain very good and very bad men on the earth. A part of this is what blend of celestial, terrestrial, and telestial types of spirits God sends to the earth at any given time. (See "Election and Reprobation" by Brigham Young and Willard Richards in Joseph Smith, *History of the Church,* 4:256–66.)

An example of how the Lord gently intervenes in historical events was his instruction to Nephi to write two records that we have named the Small Plates of Nephi and the Large Plates of Nephi. Later, he instructed Mormon to include "this small account" (the Small Plates of Nephi) with his abridgment of the Large Plates of Nephi for the same period. So, when Martin Harris lost the translation of the abridgment of the Large Plates of Nephi, which covered the first four hundred years or so, Joseph Smith was instructed not to retranslate the abridgment of the Large Plates of Nephi for that period but instead to start over with the Small Plates of Nephi. Thus the Lord frustrated the plans of scheming, diabolical men and shaped history in such a manner as to make the Book of Mormon possible. (See D&C 10:6–30.) In turn, the Book of Mormon has had immeasurable influence in shaping the history of modern times. And it will have greater influence in the future. Its content and modern influence is a witness to all mankind that the Lord does not leave history to chance and yet does not destroy the agency of his children.

The Lord knows and understands individuals. He has sovereign power over all nations; but he exercises his power with discretion and wisdom. His foreknowledge frequently falsifies man's predictions. For instance, it points up serious flaws in the Marxist philosophy of history and in the Marxist dialectic. Hence even though the Communists are in Latin America in precisely the places and ways Marx and Lenin predicted they would be, they will finally fail. Power-seeking men do not know the end of all things, but the Book of Mormon reveals that God does. The Lord has set in motion the plans to preserve freedom and his Church. We may pay a terrible price for having stood by doing nothing while disaster overtook us; but the Lord will save what he wants to save. (See Ether 8:22–26.) Babies will be born who will become the men and women needed to save the righteous remnant with the help of the Lord. He gave us the Founding Fathers, and he will give us whatever it takes to preserve the kingdom of God and establish Zion. (See Mark E. Petersen, *The Great Prologue* [Salt Lake City: Deseret Book Co., 1976].)

Take-off Passage

1 Nephi 9.

Other Passages

1 Nephi 13; 22:7–12; 2 Nephi 10:10–17; Omni 1:30; Words of Mormon 1:1–7; Alma 18:32; 3 Nephi 21:4; Mormon 8:22; Isaiah

40:8–22; Acts 17:26; Joseph Smith—History 1:33; Doctrine and Covenants 1:1–7; 3:1–6; 10:1–46. (Study Joseph Fielding Smith's books *The Progress of Man* [Genealogical Society of Utah, 1936] and *Essentials in Church History* [Salt Lake City: Deseret Book Co., 1969].) (See also GSJS.)

Study Questions

1. How are prophets and other great men evidence that history is not left entirely to chance?
2. How do dictators, kings, and other prominent people affect history? How do the places and times of their birth have a bearing on how they affect history?
3. What did Paul mean when he said that God "determined the times before appointed and the bounds of their habitation?" (Acts 17:26 and context.) How does this affect history?
4. What effect did the selling of Joseph into Egypt have upon the future history of Israel and Egypt?
5. How did the preservation of Moses by his mother affect history?
6. How do evil men unwittingly bring about the Lord's purposes? Why did the Lord cast the devil out to this earth instead of to some place where he couldn't tempt us?
7. What miracles of the Exodus would not have occurred if the pharaoh had been a good man instead of an extremely evil man? How could God foreknow that he would be so evil?
8. What effect has the house of Israel had on history? Would that have happened if the Lord had not created and shaped them as a peculiar people?

The Lord Is the Author and Editor of the Book of Mormon • AE •

It is generally understood that the editor of a newspaper is the one who really has the final say as to what others may or may not print in his paper; and he must be responsible for it. Likewise we believe that authors are responsible for what appears in their books, regardless of who helps them or from what sources the inputs come.

Looking at it this way, our Heavenly Father is the author and editor of the Book of Mormon. His Son, Jesus Christ, and his prophets obeyed his will and worked to bring about his eternal purposes. Nephi, Mormon, Moroni, and Joseph Smith were instruments used by him to bring the book into existence in our time. It was done in his way, and to accomplish what he wanted. He designed and controlled what would be included. He protected it from men and the elements for fourteen hundred years after Moroni had finished his work. He prepared the means for its translation and publication. And he has promised that he will continue to prepare the way for it to be successful in accomplishing his eternal purposes.

The question everyone must ask and answer himself or herself about the Book of Mormon is this: Was Joseph Smith the author and editor or was God the author and editor?

Take-off Passage

1 Nephi 9:5–6.

Other Passages

1 Nephi 6:4–6; 1 Nephi 19:16; 2 Nephi 3:19; 5:29–32; 33:10–15; Enos 1:13; Words of Mormon 1:1–9; Alma 37:1–24; 3 Nephi 26:12; 28:25; Mormon 6:6; 8:4–22; Mormon 9:31–34; Moroni 10:2–7; D&C 3:1–11; 10.

Study Questions

1. See if you can list ten reasons why it would make a difference if Joseph Smith was the author and editor of the Book of Mormon instead of the Lord?
2. In what ways is Joseph Smith the author? the editor?
3. Why did Joseph Smith list himself as "author and proprietor" in the first edition?
4. What difference does it make to you if the Lord is the author and editor instead of Joseph Smith?

The Book of Mormon Is Proof of the Divine Birth of Jesus • DBJ •

One of the principal ways of attacking the Bible is by denying the divinity of Jesus Christ. (See ABT.) The references in this section show that his birth happened as the New Testament gospels describe it: a virgin conceived by the power of the Holy Ghost, and the divine Son she bore was the Only Begotten of the Father. This holy person, Jesus, had power over death because of the seeds of immortality within him. He could have put off his death forever because of the divinity inherited from his Father. He was able to die because of his mother, who was as mortal as the rest of us. He also inherited from his Father the title of Father. He was a God who came among men to perform an act that only a God could perform. (See Alma 34:10.)

Take-off Passage

1 Nephi 11:12–34.

Other Passages

1 Nephi 10:4–14; 19:6–10; Mosiah 3:5–8; 15:1–9 (see also chapters 13–16); Alma 7:7–12; 34:10–14; 3 Nephi 11:3–12; Isaiah 7:14; Matthew 1:23; Luke 1:34, 35.

Study Questions

1. How does your belief concerning the divine birth of Jesus affect your belief concerning the atonement of Christ?
2. What line of reasoning would you use to show that faith in the Book of Mormon increases faith in Christ?
3. What difference does it make whether Mary was a virgin when she conceived Jesus?
4. How does your belief concerning the divine birth of Jesus affect your feelings about the moral teachings in the Bible?
5. Why would it be impossible to accept the Bible as a religious authority if you rejected the Bible doctrine that Jesus was the divine Son of God?
6. How does the doctrine of dispensations of the gospel help explain the many claims among "primitive" people that their early leaders or early prophets were descendants of the gods?
7. How does the doctrine of the "immaculate conception" (that Mary was not tainted by "original guilt") relate to the doctrine of depravity? Why do Latter-day Saints reject these doctrines?

The Book of Mormon Bears Witness to the Doctrine of the Restoration • R •

One reason why the Lord went to such great pains to prepare and preserve the Book of Mormon was that it was to be the keystone in the arch of the restoration of the gospel and the true Church in this last dispensation. In other words, it is the proof of such things as Joseph Smith's prophetic calling, modern revelation, modern authority, the truth of the Doctrine and Covenants and the Pearl of Great Price, and the truth of the Bible as far as it has been transmitted to us correctly. Those are all necessary stones in the arch, and they are held together and in place by the Book of Mormon, "the keystone of our religion," as Joseph Smith named it. Anyone who questions any of these building blocks can resolve his doubt by finding out for himself, by revelation, that the Book of Mormon is true.

But in addition to this keystone aspect of the Book of Mormon, by which it bears witness to the developments of the Restoration, it contains the *doctrine* of the Restoration. That is, it bears witness to the Bible doctrine of an apostasy and a restoration by teaching and clarifying the great Bible doctrines and prophecies on the subject. Through the Book of Mormon the Lord restored many of the "plain and precious things" that were lost from the Bible. He revealed therein that the Restoration would take away the "stumbling blocks" of the Dark Ages and of the Reformation. He revealed the name and mission of Joseph Smith in such a manner as to assure us that Joseph would never become a "fallen prophet," as some apostates have supposed. In the great parable of the tame and wild olive trees, which was lost from the Old Testament, God outlines his plans for the ultimate restoration of all Israel. Thus the Book of Mormon contains a very important and complete doctrine of restoration. (A fragment of this parable of the tame and wild olive trees was saved by Paul in Romans 11:15–25. This fragment has puzzled the Bible scholars for many years because they can see that Paul was quoting from someone else whose writings they do not have.)

Take-off Passage

1 Nephi 13:30–42.

Other Passages

1 Nephi 9; 2 Nephi 3:6–24; 26:16–18; 27; 29:1–14; Jacob 5–6; Words of Mormon; 3 Nephi 21:1–11; 29; Mormon 7:8–9; 8:12–35; Ether 4:14–19; 5; Moroni 10:24–27; Daniel 2:44; Acts 3:19–21; Ephesians 1:10; Doctrine and Covenants 3; 20:1–32; 65. (See also PI, CR, GSJS, and ADC.)

Study Questions

1. How do the prophecies in 1 Nephi 22:15–20, 3 Nephi 26:1–11, and Ether 13:6–9 give you hope, comfort, and assurance about the future?

2. After reading 1 Nephi 10:17–22; 2 Nephi 10:24; 25:23; 31:5–20; Mormon 9:7–10; Matthew 7:13–14; Ephesians 2:7–10; and Revelation 22:19–21, describe how the stumbling blocks of the Reformation were taken away by the Restoration.

3. What beliefs and movements in the Reformation prepared the way for the Restoration?

4. What role was played by the doctrine of the separation of church and state, which began to gain momentum in the period following the Reformation?

5. What has a person implied about his belief in the sovereignty of God when he says the prophets violate the doctrine of separation of church and state by offering political and economic advice? What is he saying about his belief in prophets?

6. How would the concept of separation of church and state fail in practice if it meant that churches cannot try to influence politics?

7. Why would the Restoration grind to a halt if our enemies succeeded in eliminating the freedoms that remain of those that were won by the blood and toil of our Founding Fathers and other patriots?

The Book of Mormon Proves the Authenticity of the Bible Text • ABT •

Because the Latter-day Saints say that the Bible is true "as far as it is translated correctly" (Articles of Faith 1:8), we are accused of rejecting the Bible. Yet every attempt at a better translation, every search for a new manuscript, every investigation into the Dead Sea Scrolls and similar discoveries is an admission that we are right in taking that position. The LDS Church makes no real attack on the authenticity of the Bible; but there are those who do.

Those who attack the Bible are those wolves in sheeps' clothing who use the so-called critical-historical approach. Their attack on the Bible falls into four main areas: (1) they reject the divinity of Jesus Christ; (2) they humanize and rationalize away the miracles; (3) they teach that there were two or more contributors to the book of Isaiah, and that much of the book was written in the sixth century B.C. instead of in Isaiah's day, the eighth century B.C.; (4) they claim that the five books of Moses (Pentateuch) were not written by Moses and that it was a collection of myths and traditions reduced to writing as much as a thousand years after Moses' day. These "higher critics," who pose as Bible scholars, believe in organic evolution; and since, as they believe, modern man evolved from primitive ape-like men, his religion also must have evolved from primitive superstitions of the sort ape-men would believe.

While the Book of Mormon teaches that many plain and precious things were taken out of the Bible, it also teaches that what is left is substantially true. Elsewhere in this book there are sections on the corruption of the Bible by change and by deletion, indicating the extent of corruption. (See COBC and COBD.) There also are several sections proving the truths of Bible teachings, such as those that deal with the divinity of Christ. (See CGOT, MLM, and EPC.) In this section, scriptures are offered to substantiate the truth of the Bible by supporting the truth of miracles, by showing the fact that there was only one Isaiah and that he wrote before 600 B.C., and by proving Moses' authorship of the Pentateuch.

The deutero-Isaiah (second Isaiah) theory asserts that chapters 1–39 of Isaiah were written by one person and chapters 40–66 by another later person. In the references cited below, it will be seen that the brass plates contained parts of Isaiah from each of these two halves and that all these quotations are attributed to the same person, Isaiah. (The brass plates were brought from Jerusalem by Lehi and his family. They are an accurate and more nearly complete "Old Testament" down to Jeremiah.)

Most of the other passages are self-explanatory. (See also 2N. The reader must always remember that these sections are not complete. They are only a start and an indication of where to look and how to study.)

Take-off Passage

1 Nephi 13:38–42.

Other Passages

1 Nephi 5:10–13; 13:20–29; 14:18–27; 17:26–32, 40–42; 20, 21; 2 Nephi 7, 8, 12–24, 25:1–8, 18–20; 26, 27; Mosiah 3:5, 6; 13, 16; Helaman 8:11–15; 3 Nephi 12–14, 16:17; 20:11; 22–25; Mormon 8:23; Ether 4:16; Matthew 27:52, 53.

Study Questions

1. How can you use the Book of Mormon to restore someone's faith and confidence in the Bible? Write a dialogue to illustrate how you would do it.
2. How can you use the Book of Mormon to show someone that Christ was not just a great moral teacher?
3. How does the Book of Mormon prove that all of Isaiah was written earlier than many scholars have said? Outline your argument.
4. How many Bible miracles does the Book of Mormon prove really happened? Start a list of them.
5. How can you use the ideas and principles presented in ABT to do effective missionary work?

The Book of Mormon Teaches That America Must Make a Decision About Christ • ADC •

The Book of Mormon reveals that the Gentiles must make a decision about Christ. Apparently this especially applies to the "mighty nation among the Gentiles," which always has been interpreted by the prophets to refer to the United States of America. These Gentiles are told that, if they accept him, they will have safety and prosperity; but if they reject him, they are to be brought down into spiritual and temporal captivity to the devil. Further, they are told that acceptance of the Book of Mormon is proof of acceptance of Christ, and rejection of the Book of Mormon is proof of rejection of Christ.

It seems that the prophets of the Book of Mormon were quite

certain that the decision, in general, would be negative and that the calamities therefore would fall upon the Gentiles. But the faithful have been promised some protection. At least, the faithful will be preserved as a group. The Church will not be destroyed, even though it will be cleansed. The kingdom will be here when the King comes. If necessary a second republic will be established if this one crumbles.

Take-off Passage

1 Nephi 14:6–7.

Other Passages

1 Nephi 22:17–19; 2 Nephi 10:10–17; 27:1–3; 30:10; 3 Nephi 16:7–10; 20:27; Ether 2:7–12; 8:23–26; Doctrine and Covenants 1:17, 18; 45:66–75; 84:49–53; 87; 101:81–90; 135; 136:32–36.

Study Questions

1. Explain why a believer in the Book of Mormon would think that the majority of the American people have rejected Christ.
2. What actions and counsel of the General Authorities of the Church show that they expect physical calamities to befall the United States if its people do not turn to Christ?
3. What is the best thing you can do to prepare for the troubles that lie ahead?
4. Discuss as many situations as you can in which nations have suffered physical judgments from God when they have turned their backs on Christ. What cases are told about in the Book of Mormon? in the Bible?
5. In the Book of Mormon account, why does material prosperity tend to follow the righteous but not the wicked? What lesson does this have for moderns? What do governments have to do with this question?
6. What rewards for righteousness are better than prosperity?

The Book of Mormon Teaches That the World Sometimes Suffers the Judgments of God • WJ •

Some have thought that because God says, "Thou shalt not kill"

(Exodus 20:13), he, too, cannot or would not pass a sentence of death upon anyone or otherwise execute judgment or punishment upon mankind. It must be remembered that the same God who said "Thou shalt not kill" commanded men to inflict capital punishment upon their fellowmen for certain grievous sins, such as murder, adultery, strong addiction to alcohol, abortion, idolatry, and homosexuality. And he gave both commandments in the same document, the Pentateuch, which contains the Ten Commandments, the law of Moses, and the civil code God gave Moses. It also should be remembered that God knows best when men are better off dead than alive. One who truly believes in the goodness of God and in life after death is not much disturbed by this. Those who have studied the scriptures and profane history know that infinitely more are killed when the judgments of God come down on nations than would have been killed by the proper use of capital punishment. War, plagues, and natural and social calamities rarely distinguish between the innocent and the guilty. And many of them are the natural result of disobedience to God's laws.

None of the above is to be construed as advocating that capital punishment should be applied as extensively as in the time of Moses.

The testimonies in the passages offered here and in many other places show that God *does* execute judgment on the world. The Bible and the Book of Mormon support each other in this doctrine.

Take-off Passage

1 Nephi 17:33–46.

Other Passages

1 Nephi 4:12, 13; Jacob 4:13–16; Alma 37:28–31; Helaman 12:3–26; 3 Nephi 8:5–25; 9:1–12; Mormon 6:16–22; Ether 8:20–26; Genesis 19:24; Exodus 12; Matthew 23:34–39; Doctrine and Covenants 88:94–104.

Study Questions

1. Why was it right for God to pass the death sentence on Laban and on nations when it would be wrong for men to do the same?
2. What does the Book of Mormon advise you to do to prepare for world judgments?

3. Why is a person denying the truth of the Book of Mormon when he says it was Nephi's idea (not God's) that Laban should be killed? (See also questions in previous topic, ADC.)

The Book of Mormon Teaches That No Flesh Can Be Justified by Obedience to Law • NFJ •

A person is justified in his course of action if it gets him to the goal he truly is seeking. Thus, if a person only wants to be rich, he would be justified in following any practice he could get away with, scrupulous or unscrupulous, that would make him rich. But if he has other goals that interfere with being unscrupulous, then he is justified only in seeking riches in honest pursuits.

The goal of a knowledgeable and properly motivated Christian is to arrive at the judgment bar of God in a clean state so that he can escape punishment and dwell forever with God in his kingdom. The thing that can keep him from reaching this goal is sin. Justice demands that every sin be accounted for and paid for. He has no way of paying for his own sins except by suffering great anguish and being cast out of God's presence. His good deeds will not pay for his bad deeds. If a man goes through one red light, but stops at ten thousand red lights, the law has a claim on him for going through that one red light—that is, if the law catches him. God's law always catches us, and we all sin to some degree. And his justice works the same way as our traffic laws work.

When Lehi said that "by the law is no flesh justified," he was saying that, if you are counting on your obedience to law to pay for your disobedience to law, then you won't be justified in that plan of action. It will not get you to the judgment bar clean and free from punishment. But there is an escape. It is called the atonement of Christ. He paid for every sin of every person. Therefore, he has the right to forgive us on certain terms. These terms are a broken heart and a contrite spirit, obedience to the principles and ordinances of the gospel, and endurance to the end of this mortal life.

Take-off Passage

2 Nephi 2:5–10.

Other Passages

2 Nephi 10:24; 25:23–28; 31:19; Enos 1:5–8; Mosiah 13:28–35; Alma 22:14–16; 24:10; 36:17–26; 42:12–16; Matthew 3:9; 7:21–23; Romans 3:19, 20; 4:15; 5:8–11; Galatians 2:16; 5:14–18; Ephesians 2:8–10; Titus 3:1–8; Doctrine and Covenants 20:30.

Study Questions

1. What principles and hopes of the gospel would we have to give up if all we had were the moral and ethical teachings of the world in general?
2. Upon whose merits must you rely before the judgment bar? Why? (See Helaman 14:13.)
3. Why would it be impossible for a person to be saved without Christ even if he never broke a single commandment?
4. What does it mean to say a person is *justified?*
5. What is meant by the "ends of the law" and the "ends of the atonement?"
6. Under what circumstances are works justified? (See D&C 88:14–35.)

The Power of the Devil Is Real • PD •

The devil is a real person with a real power that is the counterfeit or opposite of good. This is the power of evil. The devil is an enemy of God. He seeks the misery of all mankind. He has the ability to tempt people who have reached the age of accountability if they let him. The Book of Mormon calls this "listing" to obey him. Christ is the power we need to reject Satan. That is, if we exercise the will to live righteously and seek his help, Christ will give us his Spirit and power. We are free to follow Christ, the good shepherd, or the devil, who is the hireling or the wolf, who doesn't care for the flock.

Take-off Passage

2 Nephi 2:15–18, 28.

Other Passages

1 Nephi 22:26; 2 Nephi 2:27–29; 9:8, 9; 28 (especially verses 21, 22); 20; 32:8, 9; Mosiah 2:32–39; 3:6; Alma 5:39–42; 30:53; 37:33;

Helaman 14:30, 31; 3 Nephi 18:18; Matthew 4:1–11; Luke 22:31; 1 John 4:1, 2; 2 John 7–11; Joseph Smith 2:15–17; Doctrine and Covenants 29:36–40; 50:1–5, 14–23; 52:14; 76:25–30.

Study Questions

1. List some concepts that the devil taught Korihor which are still being taught by many people today.
2. Why would the devil want us to believe that he does not exist?
3. How does the devil's misery affect our lives?
4. How does one overcome the power of the devil?
5. How did the devil, whether wittingly or unwittingly, serve the purposes of the Lord when he talked Eve into partaking of the forbidden fruit? Why is this not to the devil's credit?
6. What was the reason the Lord banished Satan and his "angels" to this earth instead of to some place where he couldn't tempt us?

Fall of Adam • FA •

Probably most speculation about the Fall is useless, for the truth or error of this speculation cannot be made known in this life by human means. A good discussion of the Fall need go no further than the Book of Mormon goes. This consists principally of explaining (1) that the Fall came about as a result of a transgression by free agents, (2) that it introduced sin and death into an erstwhile immortal world, (3) that an atonement has been made so that no one will be able to blame his fate on the Fall, and (4) that the Fall served a great purpose in God's plan for his children.

Rejection of the doctrine of the Fall is now almost universal throughout the world. In its place we are taught that man is the product of organic evolution. Organic evolution is the basic doctrine underlying humanism, socialism of almost every variety, fascism, and many other ideas prevalent in the world today. Rejection of organic evolution and acceptance of the fall of Adam would be fatal to those ideas.

Organic evolution is based on three ideas:

1. Uniformitarianism. This is the doctrine that all things are happening at about the same rate as they have on the average for the past millions or billions of years. While it accommodates minor and local catastrophes, uniformitarianism denies such cataclysms as the

Flood and the rapid division of the land mass into separate continents that, according to the Bible, is supposed to have occurred during and shortly after the Flood.

2. The principle of common descent. This is the doctrine that all life on this planet has a common ancestor or common ancestors. Life, evolutionists say, commenced hundreds of millions of years ago when certain hydrocarbons combined into microscopic forms thought to be precursors of life. Yet the probabilities (odds) of this happening at all, and of becoming self-perpetuating, are so astronomical as to be beyond the comprehension of mortal man. Indeed, according to mathematicians who have figured it out, it would take thousands of pages to list the zeroes in the odds figures involved in these beginning events. It requires far more credulity to believe it than to believe the story of the Garden of Eden.

3. The principle of natural descent. This principle states that all life has been mortal from that first fraction of a cell life to the present complex forms of life that exist today.

If any one or all of the above three tenets of the religion of humanism is false, organic evolution is false. And, therefore, if the Fall occurred, organic evolution is false; because the doctrine of the Fall is antithetical to all three.

Take-off Passage

2 Nephi 2:17–25.

Other Passages

2 Nephi 9:6; Mosiah 3:19; 16:3–8; Alma 12:21–27; 22:13; 42:2–7; Helaman 14:16; Mormon 9:12, 13; Ether 3:2; Romans 5:14–20; Moses 4:6–32; 5:4–11; 6:46–62; Doctrine and Covenants 20:18–20; 29:40–43.

Study Questions

1. What basic concepts of the Fall oppose the ideas of common and natural descent in the theory of organic evolution?

2. If you accept the scriptural teaching that a great part of the mission of Christ was to overcome the effects of the Fall, why could you not accept the theory of organic evolution as fact?

3. Why is it a waste of time to try to reconcile the scriptures with the theories of men of any given period of time?

4. How does the fall of Adam affect people as individuals and the human race as a whole?

5. Why is it impossible for people to prove or disprove any explanation of the Creation without the help of revelation?

6. According to the scriptures, what was the state of "all things" when they were first created? How long would they have remained in this state if there had been no Fall?

It Is Necessary to Overcome the Flesh If We Wish to Be Saved • F •

Paul in 1 Corinthians 2 and Benjamin in Mosiah 3:19 both taught that there is a potential in each of us for a "natural man" or "man of flesh" to gain the ascendancy and develop an appetite for sin. This "natural man" must be displaced by a "spiritual man" or reborn person if we wish to escape from carnal desires. (Used in this sense in the scriptures, of course, the word *man* has always meant both man and woman.) All Christians who are Christian in the biblical sense believe that the fallen flesh is some kind of a problem to the soul of man, and that this fallen flesh must be overcome or ruled by the spirit in man. "For to be carnally minded is death; but to be spiritually minded is life and peace." (Romans 8:6.)

As Paul continued this sermon on carnality (*carnal* means "flesh") and spirituality, he explained to the Roman Saints that the way to overcome the flesh was through Christ and by the help of the Spirit.

The problem of good and evil in mankind has always been a subject of debate among philosophers, theologians, and educators. Some solve it by denying that the problem exists. Others maintain that it is environmentally induced and would not exist if we gave the government and the scientific community enough money and power to redirect society into benign pursuits. Horace Mann declared that if every child were educated in public schools, violence and crime would disappear. No matter how each new generation increases the educational budget, many educators claim that not enough is being spent on teachers, counselors, administrators, facilities, and special programs. "Give us enough money and we will be able to solve the problem." The theory is that violence is primarily the result of unemployment, and unemployment is the result of lack of education, and lack of education is the result of inadequate taxes to support public education.

Another explanation of good and evil puts forth the claim that evil is entirely a matter of heredity and nothing can be done about it This was the basis of Taylor Caldwell's novel, *Wicked Angel,* and it has been explored in many novels. Cain was a son of perdition and apparently inherently evil. How can he be explained by heredity or environment? Of course, he cannot unless you reject the Bible account of the origin of man and accept organic evolution, which would give Cain millions of human and sub-human ancestors. The Pearl of Great Price explains him by stating that he was a son of perdition before he was born. (Moses 5:24.)

There are, of course, other explanations of the problem of good and evil. And, as with most of those explored above, there usually is some truth in them. But the Book of Mormon solution (which is also the Bible solution) is the only true and adequate solution; all others are so mixed with error as to make them false. This solution is that, to the extent that evil can be eliminated, it only can be eliminated when sinners overpower the flesh. Christ, his Spirit, and the gospel are the tools that must be used. That is, we must believe in and accept Christ. We must obtain his Spirit, the gift of the Holy Ghost, by obeying the gospel. Then, through constant strivings against temptation, we can gain the ascendancy over the flesh. No one can simply be educated into righteousness in even the best of state schools. Even the most powerful governments, with unlimited taxing power and wealth to tax, could not, by creating social programs, develop a righteous society.

It is not that the flesh has a separate life of its own. We are made up of an intelligence that was "organized" into a spirit in the premortal spirit world. This spirit was born into a mortal body that was conceived by our mortal parents, who passed on the fall of Adam to us. Because of the Fall and because of the presence of the devil and his angels, this body and spirit can be led into sin. However, we can withstand temptation. We can say no to the devil. We can improve in our ability to say no. We have the light of Christ, which is the power of truth and the means of leading to right and truth. We can gain a second spiritual help, the Holy Ghost. Then we have even greater light and truth, greater power to select and obey the best principles. This life is essentially a test to see if we will follow the flesh or follow the light that God has given us to lead us to Christ and salvation.

Take-off Passage

2 Nephi 2:29.

Other Passages

1 Nephi 19:6; 2 Nephi 2:16; 4:17; 10:24; 3 Nephi 28:9; Ether 3:2; Doctrine and Covenants 1:19; 38:11; 93:4; 101:26; 112:23; Abraham 3:18–28; JS—H 1:28; Romans 7:13–25; 8:1–18; Galatians 5:15–26; 1 Peter 2:11.

Study Questions

1. Why is it impossible to have a simple explanation for the good and evil in each person?
2. On the other hand, what explanations for good and evil are common to all people?
3. Why can evil people come out of the same environments as good people?
4. What is the Book of Mormon solution to the problem of the "flesh"?
5. What did Christ have in common with all of us that made him subject to pain, temptation, and similar mortal conditions? What did he have that was not common to the rest of us and which made it possible for him to rise above every temptation?
6. What bearing does our handling of the "flesh" have on our ultimate destiny?

The Mission and Name of the Great Seer, Joseph Smith, Were Prophesied Thousands of Years Before He Was Born

• GSJS •

If that heavenly fire, the Holy Ghost, has come down into your very bones and told you the Book of Mormon is true, and if you have studied the book carefully, you will know certain things about Joseph Smith: (1) He was known on earth by the name of Joseph nearly four thousand years ago. (2) He was a descendant of that Joseph, son of Jacob, who was sold into Egypt by his brethren. (3) That same Joseph, top leader in Egypt, foretold Joseph Smith's coming, his name, the name of his father, and many details of his greatness and his ministry. (4) The things which are said about the great seer, Joseph Smith, make it abundantly clear that anyone who has said that he became a fallen prophet has denied the truth of the Book of Mormon and is, himself or herself, an apostate. If we accept the Book of Mormon as the word of God, we must accept Joseph Smith and his successors and all those prophetic teachings that he gave and that are attested to by the Apostles, the Spirit, and the voice of common consent.

Take-off Passage

2 Nephi 3:6.

Other Passages

2 Nephi 3:8–11, 17–19; 4:1–2; Mosiah 8:13–18; 3 Nephi 21:8–11; Mormon 8:14–16, 25; Ether 3:21–28; Doctrine and Covenants 1:17; 5:4; 21:7; 24:7–10; 100:8–10; 135. (See also HCD and the Genesis 48 and 50 material from the Joseph Smith Translation following the Bible Dictionary in the new editions of the Bible, pp. 798–800.)

Study Questions

1. In what ways was Joseph Smith a great prophet "like unto" Moses and the Joseph who was sold into Egypt?
2. List several facts that the Joseph who was sold into Egypt knew about our dispensation of the gospel.
3. If you want to know when someone is teaching you false doctrine, how can you use the record of Joseph and the record of Judah in solving your problem? Give examples.
4. How does this subject (GSJS) help you understand the fallacies in the claims of the sects and cults that have broken away from The Church of Jesus Christ of Latter-day Saints? Given the truth of the Doctrine and Covenants on church courts and government, is saying that a successor of Joseph Smith became a fallen prophet any different from saying that Joseph Smith became a fallen prophet?

Nephi Taught That Those Who Put Their Trust in the "Arm of Flesh" Instead of in God Will Be Cursed • T •

In our times, maybe more than any other, people look to mankind for a solution to all their problems. They seem to think that someone else—usually "science" or "the government"—can and should take care of all their worries, all their woes, all their wants, and all their cares. Not only that, they think that scientists are smarter and more reliable than prophets on all matters of education or information about any subject whatsoever. And of course there are times when some scientists know more than some prophets about a given technical area. For instance, if you wished to know how DNA (deoxyribonucleic acid) operates in the scheme of heredity, you would go to a biochemist instead of an Apostle. Even if the Apostle were a biochemist, you would go to him as a biochemist instead of as an Apostle on that subject. There is nothing wrong with that. But if you were concerned about the constant effort of evolutionists to repeal Mendel's laws ("like begets like") in contradiction to the efforts of the Apostles to explain creation in scriptural terms, who would be your most trustworthy authority? In this case, if the consensus of the biochemists, if they disagree with the prophets, means more to you than the consensus of the Apostles, you are putting your trust in the arm of flesh instead of in God.

There are two possible ultimate authorities: God or man. No matter how you try, you cannot come up with a third. The only question is whether or not God speaks. Most men would say, "If I knew that God has spoken on any scientific or religious or political subject, I would accept it. But I don't know that he has. And there is no way I can know that he has. The prophets of the Bible were men just like me."

And that would be a true statement if all we had was the Bible and if it were true that God doesn't speak any more. Then you would be accepting men instead of God. For if God does not speak any more or is nonexistent any more, all the authorities on the Bible are just Bible "scientists." Then there is only one authority: man.

But with the advent of the Book of Mormon there is a way to discover for yourself that God has spoken again and that he will go on speaking through his prophets—and even through you, in some cases—forevermore. Therefore, with a testimony of the truth of the Book of Mormon, you are justified in trusting in God instead of in science.

Your trust in science should be limited; but your trust in God should be unlimited.

Take-off Passage

2 Nephi 4:34–35.

Other Passages

2 Nephi 4:17–20; 22:2; 28:31; Mosiah 4:6; 7:19, 33; 23:14; Alma 36:3, 27; Alma 37:32; 38:5; 58:32–37; Helaman 12:1–3; Doctrine and Covenants 1:18–19; 11:12; 84:115–116; 2 Samuel 22:3; Mark 10:24–25; 2 Corinthians 1:9–10; Ephesians 1:12–14; 1 Timothy 4:9–10. (See also MID and NEED.)

Study Questions

1. Is ignorant, struggling man going to overpower nature by himself? Is he going to bring peace, the end of suffering, the end of want? Can he produce his own immortality?
2. When should you trust science, technology, government, money, education, and natural resources to solve your problems? What guidelines has the Lord given us? Where can you find them?
3. Why is it impossible to have God and science as equal final authorities?
4. What can Christian families do to overcome the bad teaching influences in the world which impose humanism on their children? How can they reinforce the good teaching influences which only encourage pursuit of truth?
5. How does the past record of the learned world discourage you from putting your trust in it now?
6. Make a list of decisions you could make and actions you could take right now that would show absolute trust in God?

The Righteous Nephites Were Industrious • I •

From the beginning the Lord decreed that man should "earn his bread by the sweat of his brow." One reason why is that people who don't learn to work and to love work are never happy and never find fulfillment in life.

The Lord has revealed in many places that he expects his people to work. Work is an honor, a privilege, a blessing, a way of life, and a commandment of the Lord. It makes men out of boys and women out of girls. The Lord blesses and magnifies those who work honorably. His working Saints enjoy the fruits of their labors. Students discover their best talents by working hard at everything they are asked to do. Later they learn what they are happiest doing for a living by working hard at every job that comes their way.

There is no book which teaches more emphatically the value of work and the folly of idleness than the Book of Mormon.

Take-off Passage

2 Nephi 5:17.

Other Passages

2 Nephi 9:51; Jacob 2:12–19; Mosiah 2:14; 13:17; 23:5; Alma 1:26–32; 24:18; 30:32–34; Helaman 6:8–13; 4 Nephi 23–26; Doctrine and Covenants 42:42; 56:14–17; 106:3; Genesis 3:19; Matthew 25:14–29.

Study Questions

1. Under what circumstances would temporal goods be a blessing? When would they be a curse?
2. What reasons does the Lord give for blessing people temporally?
3. What does coveting have to do with this subject? Why is it not necessary to covet in order to be rich? What does coveting lead to?
4. Why does the Church encourage bishops to be judicious in giving temporal assistance?
5. What does idleness lead to in individuals and nations?

The Book of Mormon Proves the Power and the Reality of the Resurrection • PRR •

Studies and surveys have shown that the concept of the resurrection as Latter-day Saints understand it is far from being a universal Christian belief. By "resurrection," some mean the "rising" of the spirit to heaven at death. No doubt this concept springs partly from the doctrine of depravity, inherited from the Gnostics. The Gnostics taught that God is a "pure" spirit (absolute nothingness) and that all material things (flesh) are evil. But the Book of Mormon clearly teaches that there is a resurrection (or restoration of the body to the spirit) and that the power of this resurrection is in Christ.

Take-off Passage

2 Nephi 9:4–13.

Other Passages

Mosiah 15:20–26; 26:25; Alma 11:41–46; 34:10; 40:1–5; 41:2–5; Helaman 14:17; 3 Nephi 11:12–16; 23:9–13; Matthew 27:52, 53; Luke 24:36–43; John 5:25–29; Acts 24:14, 15; 1 Corinthians 15:21, 22.

Study Questions

1. What other great principles does the Book of Mormon associate with a literal life after death?

2. What doctrines about the beginnings and endings of things (eschatology) contradict the assumption of uniformity upon which organic evolution is based? (Note: If the assumption of uniformity is true, the earth has been mortal for at least four billion years and will continue to be mortal for many times that period of time. See 2 Peter 3:3–14.)

3. Why can you not believe in reincarnation and the Book of Mormon at the same time?

4. List seven important concepts about the resurrection that were taught by Book of Mormon prophets.

The Final Judgment Follows the Resurrection of All Mankind • FJR •

The subjects of the resurrection and the judgment are so important, multi-faceted, and oft-discussed in the Book of Mormon that it is well to consider them under several headings. One such heading is the interesting fact brought out by the Book of Mormon that the real judgment, the last or final judgment, does not and cannot occur until after the resurrection of all who have lived as mortals on this earth. That is, one cannot be punished for the sins he committed in the physical body until the physical body has been restored to him. True, the time one spends in hell between death and the resurrection might be called a punishment for sin, but only in the same sense that the chains of hell on earth are a punishment for sin. A person is in hell, here or hereafter, because he persists in living in sin. In other words, hell is the state of the unrepentant sinner. He is brought out of hell by the power of the resurrection to be tried and punished. If he is raised with a celestial body, there is no punishment. The rest suffer some degree of pain during the judgment and separation from God thereafter.

Take-off Passage

2 Nephi 9:15.

Other Passages

2 Nephi 9:41; Mosiah 16:10, 11; 26:23–28; Alma 5:15; 11:43; 12:12; 33:22; 40:21–26; 41:12–15; 3 Nephi 27:14; Mormon 3:20; 1 Samuel 2:3; Doctrine and Covenants 76.

Study Questions

1. Why could there not be an effective moral force and sense of justice in the world if there were no final judgment by Almighty God?
2. List several examples in this life in which men are given opportunities and responsibilities and then must account for these to the giver of the opportunities and responsibilities.
3. How does your judgment of others differ from God's judgment of us?
4. What does God expect of you in your judgment of others?
5. How does your judgment of others affect God's judgment of you?
6. Why would it be unjust if, before we were resurrected, the Lord should judge us and punish us for the deeds done in the flesh?
7. Why is it just to allow the righteous some degree of reward even before the resurrection? Upon what are these rewards based? Upon what were they based before the time of Christ?

The Book of Mormon Teaches of an Omniscient and Omnipotent Deity • OOD •

The God of Abraham, Isaac, and Jacob—who is the God of all the scriptures—is not the finite God that some rationalists have imagined. He dwells in the bosom of eternity. (See D&C 88:13.) The past, present, and future are all present with him. (See D&C 38:1–2.) So how can there be anything he does not know?

Joseph Smith said, "It is the constitutional disposition of mankind to set up stakes and bounds to the works and the ways of the Almighty. . . . I say to all those who are disposed to set up stakes for the Almighty, you will come short of the glory of God." (*Teachings of the Prophet Joseph Smith,* comp. Joseph Fielding Smith [Salt Lake City: Deseret Book Co., 3rd ed., 1942], pp. 321–22.) In addition to the scriptures below, the Book of Mormon contains many accounts of God's revealing the hearts of men to the prophets, showing his ability to pierce man to the very center with the power of his almighty intelligence.

Take-off Passage

2 Nephi 9:20.

Other Passages

Jacob 2:5; 4:8–13; Mosiah 3:5; 4:8, 9; Alma 7:13; 18:32; 26:35; 34:10; 39:8; Helaman 9:24–36, 41; Mormon 8:17; Moroni 7:22; Moses 6:61; Doctrine and Covenants 1:1–3; 88:41.

Study Questions

1. Can any man soundly question the omniscience and omnipotence of Deity without being omniscient and omnipotent himself?

2. What do the words *omniscient* and *omnipotent* mean? Can finite man really define these terms and then use his definitions as criteria for judging whether God is omnipotent and omniscient?

3. Who is in the best position to tell us the attributes of Deity—the prophets and Apostles or those who deny revelation? Why?

4. How could God reveal the history of nations and individuals without destroying the agency of man if he were not omniscient and

omnipotent? In other words, how could anything be foretold without God's being omniscient and omnipotent unless he forced us to fulfill his prophecies?

5. Why do people who deny the omniscience of God fall short of an understanding of the atonement of Christ?

The Book of Mormon Helps Us Believe in the Reality of the Final Judgment • RFJ •

When we accept the story of the coming forth of the Book of Mormon as told by the Prophet Joseph Smith, we know that, in turn, we must agree that the teachings of that book are true. It teaches the reality of the final judgment. It helps us see how Christ could be the sole judge and still perform his judgment in the presence of the Father and the Holy Ghost. We learn also that to judge means, at least in part, to rule over. Hence, we know that the Apostles of the eastern hemisphere will rule over (judge) the house of Israel. But that will be during the Millennium and in the kingdom of God. And others will judge in this sense and in the sense that all the books will be opened to our memories and knowledge—with guilt if we are guilty. But only Christ will judge us in one great simultaneous judgment when we are brought into his infinite presence. Then the bodies we are raised with will determine whether we feel pain and how much pain we will feel. Then our deeds and thoughts will condemn us if we have not repented and received the sheltering power of the atonement of Christ. This great event will take place when this earth is melted with a fervent heat at the end of the Millennium and when all have been resurrected and brought before the judgment bar of God. It will really happen. We know that, if we know that the Book of Mormon is true.

Take-off Passage

2 Nephi 9:41.

Other Passages

1 Nephi 12:9, 10; 2 Nephi 9:15, 42–46; 33:11–15; Mosiah 16:1, 2; 27:31; Alma 5:15–18; 11:43, 44; 12:12–18; 41:2–7; Mormon

9:1–6; Moroni 10:27–34; Matthew 25:31–46; John 5:22–30; Revelation 20:12–15.

Study Questions

1. What relationship exists between moral motivation and personal knowledge of a final judgment?
2. What relationships exist among the doctrines of the final judgment, the Atonement, mercy, and justice?
3. Who will escape the final judgment?
4. Who is the sole judge of mankind? Why?
5. In what way do we determine our own judgment?
6. When will every knee bow and every tongue confess?
7. Why is it impossible for telestial beings to be converted before the final judgment?
8. Why is it wrong to describe the final judgment as an endless courtroom scene with witnesses testifying and books being read out of? Where are the books "read" and "seen"?

Works Are Necessary Even Though We Are Saved by Grace • WG •

Some extreme sections of Christendom have taught that the doctrine of grace means that a person can live a life of debauchery until he or she is dying, and then, with the last mortal breath, "confess Jesus" and be saved in the same eternal bliss as those who have practiced virtue all their days. Some even have taught that, once you have "confessed Jesus," nothing you can do can make any difference. You will be saved regardless of the life you live. "Once in grace, you cannot fall." (See *Teachings of the Prophet Joseph Smith,* pp. 338ff.)

Joseph Smith reacted strongly against this concept. He used a statement of Paul's in Hebrews to show that, if you really obtained a state of grace (that is, obtained the right to be saved and exalted through the atonement of Christ), and fell from grace, you would fall into perdition. (*Ibid.*) Falling from grace, then, would be to turn your back on the "blood of the covenant" and to consider it "an unholy thing." (Hebrews 10:26–31.) On the basis of Hebrews 6:4–6 and its context, and the Hebrews 10 statement, Joseph Smith argued that you can fall from grace after coming under grace; but, if you fall from grace, you become a son of perdition. Of course, he made it clear that no one can obtain a legitimate claim to the highest rewards of the Atonement (reach a state of grace) without baptism at the hands of the priesthood of The Church of Jesus Christ of Latter-day Saints and without being sealed by the Holy Spirit of Promise.

Some Church members, after the days of Joseph Smith have gone so far as to deny that we are saved by grace at all. Rather, they have taught, we are saved by our works. They have gone even further: they have quoted Paul's statement in Ephesians 2:8–9, "For by grace are ye saved through faith; and that not of yourselves: it is the gift of God: not of works lest any man should boast," and have said that this salvation refers to the resurrection only. We know that is incorrect for two reasons: (1) Paul stated that this salvation he was talking about came through faith; and faith is not required for a resurrection. (2) Nephi taught exactly the same thing in 2 Nephi 25:23.

President David O. McKay, referring to Ephesians 2:8, said, "That statement is absolutely true." (CR, April 1957, p. 7.) But he also taught the necessity of works and ordinances along with faith and grace. The key to understanding this statement of Paul's is in the tenth verse: "For we are his workmanship, created in Christ Jesus unto good works, which God hath before ordained that we should walk in them." It is the rebirth which creates a creature who has good works. It is not the good works of the creature which creates the rebirth. Nevertheless, a rebirth follows the exercising of faith in Christ and the experiencing of a broken heart and a contrite spirit.

The confusion can be laid to rest if we always remember that our good works do not pay the demands of justice for our evil deeds. Only Christ can do this. That is why he performed his atonement. And his atonement was an act of grace because it went above and beyond the minimum demands of justice. Jesus was obligated to pay for Adam's sin, all sins committed purely because of our being in a fallen world (sins committed in ignorance); and he was obligated to bring about a resurrection as a free gift. (See Romans 5:15.) But it might be argued that he was not legally obligated to pay for the sins we commit knowingly, except in the sense that he had volunteered to do it. A host and hostess are required by convention to be kind to considerate guests. But if the host and hostess are kind to inconsiderate guests, we say they are gracious. That helps explain why Paul and Nephi taught that we are saved from the justice of God by grace, not by our good works. And it may help explain why father Lehi taught that no "flesh" is justified by the law. (See NFJ.)

But it goes even further than mere graciousness. We *can* pay for our own sins, but it would require a second spiritual death or second separation from God to do it. We can understand this better if we always remember that obedience to traffic laws, for instance, will not pay for the infractions that are seen by officers of the law, even if the number of times we obey outnumbers the times we disobey thousands to one. The same is true of other civil laws: obedience does not pay for disobedience. God's law works the same way. Only he always sees the infractions. And the payment is very severe if we wish to pay it ourselves. This is why Paul said that the wage of sin is death—spiritual death, or separation from God. Therefore the atonement of Christ was necessary. He satisfied the demands of justice for all of us so we do not have to make this terrible payment ourselves. Thus his grace brings about an act of mercy which satisfies justice.

Take-off Passage

2 Nephi 10:24–25.

Other Passages

2 Nephi 2:5–8; 11:5–7; 25:23; 31:1–20; Ether 12:41; Moroni 9:26; 10:32–34; Doctrine and Covenants 20:30–32; 76:94; Moses 6:52; John 3:16; Ephesians 2:8–10. (Most of Romans was written by Paul to explain why good works are efficacious, natural, and necessary in the life of a Saint in spite of the fact that we are saved by grace.)

Study Questions

1. Webster defines grace as "a free gift of God to man for his regeneration and sanctification." How does this definition help you to understand grace as an essential gift in the "great plan of the Eternal God?" (Alma 34:8–10.)
2. How could a Latter-day Saint use the Book of Mormon to talk about grace to a nonmember who thinks of himself or herself as being "saved"? Consider writing a dialogue to illustrate how you would do this.
3. How do the scriptures and ideas in this section show that it is unwise for anybody to assert that Paul and James disagreed on faith and works?
4. Why would Paul call all of the deeds of fallen man ("natural man" or, in other words, unregenerated man) "dead works"? What

does this have to do with Mormon's teachings that a bitter fountain cannot bring forth good water? (Moroni 7:10–11.)

The Bible Prophesies the Coming Forth of the Book of Mormon • BPBM •

On the one hand, the Bible prophecies about the Book of Mormon are a testimony to the truth of the Book of Mormon. On the other hand, the Book of Mormon is a commentary on the meaning of the Bible prophecies about the Book of Mormon. This may seem to be the same principle as a man testifying in his own behalf; but in this case, we have the means of knowing the truth of his testimony. We are not dependent on the Bible to know the truth of the Book of Mormon; and if we know that the Book of Mormon is true, we know that we have the right interpretation of Isaiah 29, for example, because 2 Nephi 26 and 27 explain it. Also, take note of the relationship of Joseph Smith—History 1:19 to Isaiah 29:13–14, and 2 Nephi 27:26 to Doctrine and Covenants 4:1 and 6:1, and 3 Nephi 15:12–24 to John 10:16, and 2 Nephi 27:15–20 to Joseph Smith—History 1:62–65. Moroni 10:27 shows that Isaiah 29:4 had reference to the Nephites. Doctrine and Covenants 27:5 shows that Ezekiel 37:16 referred to the Book of Mormon. And there are many other places where the Bible and Book of Mormon combine to refute false doctrine and eliminate disagreement. But, of course, it all becomes meaningful only after you have that divine testimony of the truth of the Book of Mormon.

Take-off Passage

2 Nephi 26:14–18.

Other Passages

2 Nephi 3:5–22; 27; Alma 46:23–27; 3 Nephi 15:12–24; Mormon 6; Moroni 10:27; Genesis 48; 49:22–26; Deuteronomy 33:13–17; Isaiah 29; Ezekiel 37:15–20; John 10:16; Joseph Smith–History 1:19, 62–66; Doctrine and Covenants 27:5.

Study Questions

1. How does the existence of four Gospels (Matthew, Mark, Luke, and John) argue for the possibility of an additional book of

scripture like the Book of Mormon? How do Deuteronomy 4:2 and 12:32 relate to our interpretation of Revelation 22:18–19? Why would anyone wish to put a muzzle on God?

2. Why would it be reasonable to expect Nephite prophets to interpret Isaiah? What book contained their record of Isaiah's writings?

3. How can you use the ideas in this section to do missionary work?

4. List ten details in the "sealed book" prophecy (Isaiah 29) that were fulfilled in the coming forth of the Book of Mormon and events related to it.

5. Find a promise in Jacob's blessing to Joseph that could not be fulfilled without modern revelation and without a book like the Book of Mormon.

6. Why didn't Jesus tell the Jews about the Nephites?

When There Are No Miracles, It Is Because There Is No Faith • NMNF •

Many Christian churches have been teaching that God established his kingdom on miracles but that miracles have ceased; miracles and inspiration are no longer needed; and the kingdom has been turned over to men. But according to the Book of Mormon, the only thing that will cause miracles to cease is a lack of faith on the part of the people.

Even though many churches have been teaching officially that miracles have ceased and that the Bible is a closed book, some of these churches have been miracle-seekers and have unofficially encouraged belief in miracles while discouraging belief in revelation other than the Bible. When we remember that everything the Holy Ghost does is revelation by definition, we can see the inconsistency of such a position; and when we remember that the Bible teaches that one must have the Spirit in order to be saved, we can see the inconsistency of teaching salvation without miracles or new revelation.

Take-off Passage

2 Nephi 28:5–6.

Other Passages

2 Nephi 26:20; Mormon 8:26; 9:7–26; Ether 12:6; Moroni 7:33–38; 10:7–26; Doctrine and Covenants 46:10–33; 84:64–74. (Study Spencer W. Kimball, *Faith Precedes the Miracle* [Salt Lake City: Deseret Book Co., 1972].)

Study Questions

1. If, as Paul said (1 Corinthians 2:11), the things of God can be understood only by the Spirit of God, why is it inconsistent to teach that there was to be no revelation after the Bible?
2. Why is it inconsistent to teach that God is kind and loving and that he answers prayers, and then teach that there is no modern revelation?
3. What happens in a spiritual rebirth that could not happen if revelation had ceased?
4. How can you use the ideas taught in this section to do more effective missionary work?
5. Why should we not publicize personal miracles in the LDS church? If we take him at his own word in the Gospels, can we say that Christ usually publicized miracles?
6. When could a conversion based on miracles be unstable?
7. Why would it be wrong for a sign-seeker to have his desires satisfied.

The God of Israel Is Affirmed by the Testimony of Two Nations • 2N •

In court, a testimony which is presented by two competent witnesses is considered more valuable than a testimony presented by one witness—especially if that one witness is testifying in his own behalf. In a sense, one could argue that all the religions of the world except that taught by The Church of Jesus Christ of Latter-day Saints have only one witness; and in each case, that witness is the religion itself. Or it might be said that each God is vouched for by each God himself. But the Book of Mormon and the Bible stand as two witnesses for the God of Abraham, Isaac, and Jacob. Although the two peoples were widely separated in location, the Book of Mormon people bore witness to the same God as did the other Israelites in

Palestine. They did not have different religions peculiar to their own times and places. They worshiped the same God, the one described in the Old and the New Testaments. How is it that these two different cultures on two widely separated continents have produced two records which testify of the same God and of each other?

Take-off Passage

2 Nephi 29.

Other Passages

2 Nephi 3:12; Alma 46:24–26; 3 Nephi 10:16, 17; 15:16–24; 16:1–7; 20:22; Ether 13:7–9; Genesis 48; Jeremiah 3:18; Ezekiel 37:15–19; John 10:16; Acts 10:34–36; Doctrine and Covenants 3:16; 20:11, 12; 42:11, 12.

Study Questions

1. How does the Book of Mormon show that the Lord remembered the nations of Joseph (Ephraim and Manasseh) the same as he did the nation of Judah?
2. If the Nephites had followed the pattern of the great non-Christian religions of the world, who would they have deified?
3. Why have people said that the Book of Mormon speaks with "a familiar spirit?"
4. How could you use this section as a help in approaching people who are not Christians?
5. Who is the God of Abraham, Isaac, and Jacob?
6. How does the rejection of Jesus by the Jews show that they have rejected the God of their fathers? How does the Book of Mormon prove that they have rejected the God of their fathers.

If You Accept Christ or the Bible, You Will Accept the Book of Mormon • CBBM •

The Book of Mormon is like a big sieve which is sifting the nations. The big jewels or nuggets that are caught by the sieve are those who really believe in Christ or the Bible—or who would if they had a chance. The "fines" or dross are the ones who reject Christ and the Book of Mormon. The Book of Mormon claims that anyone who believes the Bible or who believes in Christ will believe in the Book of Mormon. Is this true? Of course. The same Spirit bears witness. The same righteousness is required in order for the belief to grow. One ex-minister, when he had sincerely investigated the book, told Glenn Pearson, "I realized that there was not one word in the Book of Mormon which would lead anyone astray or lead one to reject Christ. In fact, it was the most Christ-loving book I had ever read."

One who believes in Christ or the Bible will believe in prayer and will love the words of Christ. The Book of Mormon contains the words of Christ, and those who pray in faith will know it is true. (See Glenn L. Pearson, *The Book of Mormon, Key to Conversion* [Salt Lake City: Bookcraft, 1963].)

Take-off Passage

2 Nephi 33:10–12.

Other Passages

1 Nephi 6; 13:38–40; 2 Nephi 3:11–12; 5:32; 26:28–29; 30:3; 3 Nephi 11:8–19; 21:1–9; Mormon 7:8–9; John 3:16–21.

Study Questions

1. How do the ideas and concepts in this section tie in with those discussed in 2N?
2. Why would it seem reasonable to expect modern Christian evangelists—and all who profess a belief in Christ—to accept the Book of Mormon? What would you tell them the Book of Mormon is? (See 2 Nephi 33.)
3. If one emphasizes the idea that the Book of Mormon is a history of some of the American Indians, how does he miss the main point of 2 Nephi 33?
4. How can you use the ideas and concepts in this section to do effective missionary work? If you really believe these ideas, how will it help you avoid disputes with nonmembers?
5. Why will no more than a love of that which is good lead to a belief in the Book of Mormon?

Jacob Taught That Riches Should Be the Second Quest If Sought at All • RSQ •

The Lord designed this life as a test. Only those who, in the judgment of the Judge, have passed the test are worthy candidates for celestial exaltation. For instance, the Lord gave us the appetite of sexual love; but only those who adequately control it and put it in proper perspective will continue to enjoy the power of procreation in the eternal worlds.

Again, the Lord has put us into a mortal world where we must seek food, clothing, and shelter to survive. This results in cupidity, covetousness, theft, greed, and other vices. It also results in virtues that are the opposite of those vices. Jacob, the brother of Nephi, tells us that only those who seek wealth "to do good—to clothe the naked, and to feed the hungry, and to liberate the captive, and administer relief to the sick and the afflicted" will be justified in their pursuit of wealth. (Jacob 2:19.)

There are also such tests as maintaining charity for one's spouse and for all the members of the Church when we see their faults up close. However, the purpose of this section is to get you to think about this problem of the need to seek wealth and yet not let this quest destroy you.

Take-off Passage

Jacob 2:17–19.

Other Passages

2 Nephi 9:30, 42, 51; Mosiah 4:14–27; Alma 1:29–32; 7:6; 39:4; 45:24; Helaman 6:1–13; 13:18–23; 3 Nephi 6:10–15; 4 Nephi 23, 43; Ether 8:15–26; Doctrine and Covenants 38:39; 56:16–17; 134:2.

Study Questions

1. What are some important things that are required of a family man that money can buy?
2. What financial policies and programs does the Church follow that would be important for a family to adopt?
3. What are at least two sides to the story of people and riches as written about in the Book of Mormon?

4. Why would the Lord want you to find the true kingdom and get a hope in Christ before seeking riches?

5. Why would it be impractical for a group of poor people to "pool their poverty" and try to establish Zion? In other words, why will it be necessary for righteous wealthy people to be involved? Why would it be impossible to establish the United Order if the government owned or controlled the means of production?

6. Why is it uncommon for bachelors to become wealthy unless they inherit their wealth? In other words, what is the place of wives and mothers in the accumulation of righteous wealth? What have women done to the place and purpose of men when they succeed in what is called the "liberation" of women? How does this tend to place enmity between men and women?

7. Who are the poor whom we must feed, clothe, and house in most cases? Why are they our first obligation?

8. What is the common excuse for not helping the "beggars," especially if they are members of our families? Why is this excuse wrong? Why will it damn us if we do not help our own?

9. Why would the Lord (section 134) say that a nation cannot exist in peace if the right to own and control private property is destroyed?

10. Why did free enterprise prevail when the Nephites were righteous and prosperous?

The Contest in Every Intelligent Mind Is Revealed Versus Human Knowledge • RVHK •

Man is at an inestimable disadvantage when pitting his knowledge against God's knowledge. In the very best of circumstances man must reason from the part (his world) to the whole (God's world); whereas God, from whom and by whom all things exist, always reveals from the whole to the part. Man must constantly extrapolate, interpolate, and guess. God knows all things. He sees things in their entirety, in their true perspective. Hence the most reliable knowledge we have is that which God reveals or has revealed through his prophets. Therefore revealed religion should be the criterion of human reason or human knowledge, rather than the reverse. A test which shows whether someone has hold of the iron rod is his attitude toward the word of God in the standard works and the words of the living oracles. If he is ashamed of the word of God because he sees that it disagrees with the consensus of the scientific community, he does not have a firm hold of the iron rod.

It is only natural for fallen man to question whether God really speaks to the prophets. That is especially so in this so-called time of "enlightenment" when we think we know so much simply because we can recite the errors of the past. Have you noticed that most people blame the western world's errors and superstitions of past centuries on the clergy of the day? They conveniently forget that, in those times, the clergy had a monopoly on education and learning. All the scientists were churchmen and all churchmen were the learned of this world, not the learned of God's world. There were no prophets among them, by their own admission. And when the church lost its monopoly on learning, the errors continued in the science of the secular world.

It may be precisely because of the history of the "making of the modern mind" that the Lord designed the Book of Mormon and its coming forth in the way he did. On the one hand, it at least *appears* that the book cannot be verified empirically. But on the other hand, the sincere seeker can verify it for himself. This verification comes by divine revelation which leaves no doubt. One of the most important parts of the whole Book of Mormon plan was that the gold plates should not be available for scientific examination. If they were, the book would cease to have the value it presently has. Then the scoffers could really have a heyday. They could argue interminably about authenticity and translation; and then, when those issues were settled, argue forever about whether it means anything to our day. Few would be converted by it. It would not be the proof of modern revelation. Its content would not be unassailable by human reason. The Church could not have been founded on it as the "keystone." It would not prove that Joseph Smith and his successors are prophets. It would just be another artifact in a mountain of artifacts.

Take-off Passage

Jacob 4:8–13.

Other Passages

1 Nephi 8:19–30; 2 Nephi 9:28, 29, 42; 28:1–6; 32:4; Jacob 7:11–20; Mosiah 12:27; Alma 12:9–11, 28–30; 30:13–18; 32:34;

36:26; Helaman 16:17, 18; Deuteronomy 29:29; John 3:16–21; 1 Corinthians 1:18–31; 2; Colossians 2:8.

Study Questions

1. What are the conditions we must meet to learn for sure that there is modern revelation and that we can rely on that revelation even if it disagrees with the scientific consensus?
2. What is the difference between how we receive revealed knowledge and scientific knowledge?
3. What are the limits that are placed upon what science can investigate?
4. What are the limits placed upon what we can learn about God's world? (See Moses 1.)
5. Why do deists and humanists prefer to believe in a god without substance or in a set of natural laws which they give the qualities of godhood? In what ways is it correct for them to call Latter-day Saints anthropomorphists? In what ways is it incorrect for them to call us anthropomorphists? How do you know that it was Gnosticism, not the Bible, that won at the Council of Nicea?
6. See if you can list three reasons why revealed knowledge must be the standard by which you judge the validity of all other knowledge.

We Can Avoid Many Errors by Taking Counsel • TC •

Counseling is a tradition, a commandment, a policy, and a way of life in the Church of Jesus Christ. Even the prophet and President of the Church has two counselors who are provided, prepared, and chosen in the wisdom of God. This presidency, in turn, may receive counsel from the Twelve. The Twelve regularly set apart stake presidents, who have two counselors to give them counsel; and stake presidents ordain bishops, who have two counselors who give them counsel. Similarly this is the practice with priesthood quorums and auxiliary organizations. And a man has a very important and intimate counselor in his wife—and vice versa. Thus the Church organization provides the full value of counsel operating from center to periphery and back again. In like manner, children must learn to take counsel from parents, parents from bishops as assisted by home teachers, bishops from stake presidents, and stake presidents from General Authorities. Poor is the person who has no counselors, and foolish is the person who does not seek counsel.

Why all this counsel? Because the Lord "counseleth in wisdom, and in justice, and in great mercy over all his works." (Jacob 4:10.) The Prophet Joseph Smith learned by hard experience that it is wise to take counsel. (Doctrine and Covenants 3:4, 7.) Part of Sidney Rigdon's undoing was that he failed to take counsel. (Doctrine and Covenants 63:55.) If we follow counsel, we will be able to establish Zion under the Lord's direction. (Doctrine and Covenants 105:37.) The pure in heart, the wise, the noble, and the virtuous will seek counsel from the prophet. (Doctrine and Covenants 122:2.) Indeed, it might be said that the acceptance or rejection of counsel by a Saint gives his duly ordained priesthood leader insight into his mind and spirit. It gives evidence of a member's attitude and response to the mind and will of God. (Doctrine and Covenants 124:118.) And it can be destructive of the spirituality of a man of learning, of riches, or of any other special interest if he reaches the state of mind or attitude in which that interest keeps him from accepting the counsel of priesthood authority. (2 Nephi 9:29.)

Take-off Passage

Jacob 4:10.

Other Passages

1 Nephi 13:38–40; 2 Nephi 3:11, 12; 5:32; 26:28, 29; Mormon 7:8, 9; John 3:16–21.

Study Questions

1. What associations can you see between this subject and the one called RVHK?

2. What associations can you see between this subject and the one called NEED?

3. How could a prospective missionary profit from making the associations suggested in questions 1 and 2 above?

4. Who was the only person who knew exactly what God wanted him to do from moment to moment? Why?

5. What is there about the rest of us which makes it impossible to know exactly what to do all the time?

6. How do the mortality and imperfection of all men relate to the taking of counsel?
7. How does counseling relate to the reception of revelation?

Every Prophet Prophesied of Christ • EPC •

One of the most significant contributions of the Book of Mormon is its verification of the little-known and almost forgotten Bible doctrine that Christ was known by every prophet from the beginning. This support of the Bible is especially significant to recent times. Following the reintroduction of the old Greek theory of organic evolution and its elevation to "religious" stature in the nineteenth century, scholars in many fields rushed to get on the bandwagon and make their disciplines conform to evolution. Even courses in textiles and cooking started with cavemen folklore. Bible scholars, anthropologists, psychologists, and sociologists, in direct and deliberate contradiction to the facts of revelation, invented the idea that religion, too, evolved. This notion has all but divested the Christian world of what little faith it once had that Jesus was known by "all the prophets . . . until John." (Matthew 11:13.)

The true significance of this passage in Matthew 11 (that every prophet until John knew and foretold of Jesus) was forgotten, and the passage was wrested by anti-Mormons to do service for the apostate idea that revelation ceased after John—and, incidentally, they sometimes let the ignorant think it referred to John the Revelator, not John the Baptist. Prophecy is the testimony of Jesus. (Revelation 19:10.) Therefore, those who "prophesied" before Jesus were seeing into the future. Those who "prophesied" about Jesus after his coming were looking back into the past. (See 1 Corinthians 13 and 14.) So John the Baptist was the cut-off point. All before him were foretellers of Jesus. And he, too, was a foreteller of Jesus until he saw the sign of the dove and heard the voice of the Father and knew for a certainty what he already believed—that the long-awaited Messiah was this very cousin of his whom he had just baptized.

Take-off Passage

Jacob 7:11, 12.

Other Passages

1 Nephi 10:4, 5; 19:10–14; 2 Nephi 11:2; Jacob 4:4, 5, 13, 14; Mosiah 13:33; Helaman 8:14–23; Ether 12:19, 20; Luke 24:25–27, 39–41; John 4:25, 29, 42; Acts; 1 Corinthians 15:1–3; Moses 7:1; Doctrine and Covenants 20:26.

Study Questions

1. When did Christianity really begin?

2. How do you know that Adam was the first prophet? What did he know about Jesus?

3. Why would Paul say that you should seek the gift of prophecy above all the other gifts of the Spirit? (1 Corinthians 14:1. Incidentally, he was not saying that the gift of prophecy was to be preferred above charity, which he was listing not as a spiritual gift but as an acquired quality of the soul. The gifts of the Spirit belong only to this life; but charity endures forever.)

4. Since the biblical meaning of *prophecy* is "testimony of Jesus" (Revelation 19:10; 1 Corinthians 14:1), how do you suppose the word *prophecy* picked up the meaning of foretelling or predicting?

5. Presuming you could answer number 4 above, how does this help you see the fallacy in the theory that Christianity evolved from the fetish religions of so-called primitive man?

6. How does EPC and its Bible cross-references support the Book of Mormon claim that plain and precious things have been taken from the Bible?

The Anti-Christs of the Book of Mormon Taught Many Things That Are Now Taught by Humanists • H •

By Joseph Smith's day the idea of an antichrist had evolved into the idea of an Anti-Christ. The word *antichrist* is the Bible term for the false teachers in the Church who taught a false Christ instead of a true Christ. The Greek preposition *anti,* roughly translated, means *instead of.* It also carries the meaning of "face to face" or mirror image. The image in the mirror, looking back at you, is face to face with you. It looks like you. Yet it has no substance. It is a counterfeit of you, in a sense. It only appears to be you. So when John in his epistles spoke of antichrists, he was speaking of the belief of the Gnostics that God is a substanceless spirit rather than a resurrected being. (See 1 John 2:18–22; 4:1–3; 2 John 1:7.) Such a god is like the image in the mirror—really nothing, a counterfeit. Through the centuries thereafter, the term *antichrist* became *Anti-Christ,* and by Joseph Smith's day it referred to those who opposed Christ. Thus during World War II there was a lot of speculation about whether Hitler was the antichrist (or Anti-Christ). Of course, that was an error. The antichrist of the Bible came, as John said, in his day, and was the doctrine of the spirit god, which became the "Triune God" adopted at the Council of Nicea. This apostate doctrine taught that the Father, the Son, and the Holy Ghost were one God at the same time they were three and were totally without substance or form.

On the surface it would seem that the Nephite Anti-Christs—Sherem, Korihor, Nehor, and others—were not antichrists of the Bible variety. But they had a lot in common with the Bible variety. For instance, they came out of the true Church. In other words, they were apostates always. They were never Lamanites, though they led some Lamanites into the same errors. And they were deceivers and liars like the antichrists that Paul and John condemned. If we look further, we discover that the Book of Mormon Anti-Christs shared many characteristics with modern humanists.

Most humanists don't call themselves humanists, just as Bible antichrists did not call themselves antichrists. (Book of Mormon Anti-Christs, on the other hand, denied Christ openly.) But all modern humanists reject Christ either openly or by divesting him of his godhood and by relegating him to the stature of humanity. At best, they think of him as a great moral teacher who was deified by his followers. The reason why humanism is called humanism is that the humanists consider man to be the ultimate. They put man in the place of God. Of course, most of them deny that; but their teachings and actions betray them.

One way to understand humanism is to compare it with the true gospel of the Bible and the Book of Mormon. This shows God to be the supreme power in the universe, and the Father and the Son to be two separate, resurrected beings. It shows that the Father and the Son are omnipotent (all-powerful) and omniscient (all-knowing) and have the power to act everywhere at once if necessary. (Paul said that Jesus was "the brightness of [the Father's] glory, and the express image of his person." [Hebrews 1:3.]) Furthermore, it shows that the Father and the Son reveal their will to mankind through prophets.

This revelation takes many forms that are all valid and real and convey true information in a manner that it can be understood.

Humanists, in general, accept the idea of a god; but to them he is a force (sometimes called "evolution" or "natural law") that is everywhere in the universe. He is not personal or embodied. He might just be called "the law." There are those who believe in the Father and the Son as two separate, resurrected beings but who think of them as subservient to the law rather than masters of the law. Apparently they visualize the gods as super-scientists in heavenly laboratories, ever seeking truth. They do not accept Lehi's statements in 2 Nephi 2 and Joseph Smith's in Doctrine and Covenants 88:36–44, which clearly teach that, without God, the law could do nothing. Indeed, God is the giver and upholder of the law.

By definition, God is the most powerful thing or being. Hence to humanists the law is God; but to Christians the Father and the Son are God. And they are united and are equal in power and purpose.

Furthermore, humanists do not believe in prophets and revelation. To them, revelation is the greatest thinking of the greatest minds. And their authority is the consensus of the scientific community. They accept men like Marx, Freud, Darwin, Dewey, Nader, and Sagan above Moses, Isaiah, Joseph Smith, Abraham, and Paul. To a great extent, they make each man his own god and prophet. Together with Sherem, Nehor, and Korihor, they say, "There is no Christ. You cannot know things to come. You say and believe such things because you are irrational or superstitious. Every man fares according to the genius of the creature. It is vain to expect knowledge and temporal blessings from this Jesus you have invented. Nothing you do is evil. It is natural to follow the appetites of the flesh. You can't help what you are. Just do 'your thing' and, when you die, that will be the end of everything."

Take-off Passage

Jacob 7:2–20.

Other Passages

1 Nephi 11:35; 12:18; 14:13; 2 Nephi 9:28–29, 39–43; Alma 1:2–6; 10:14–16; 30; Helaman 2:4–5; 16:15–21; 3 Nephi 29; Doctrine and Covenants 46:7; 50:13–22; Romans 1:18–32 (note verse 25); 1 Corinthians 2. (See also KR, CR, NEED, and D.)

Study Questions

1. Why would you consider the feminist movement, the consumer advocate movement, and the environmentalist movement humanistic endeavors as they are presented by the world? How do these movements differ when they are motivated by Christian beliefs and feelings?
2. What common lies did Sherem, Nehor, and Korihor share about the source of their motivations, ideas, and teachings? What other lies or mistakes did they share?
3. What modern belief about the origin and nature of man is shared by all modern humanists? What effect does this have upon morality?
4. In what way is organic evolution absolutely essential to the philosophical soundness and the success of communism, fascism, and all types of socialism or Marxism?
5. List some teachings of Marx, Freud, Dewey, and their followers which are similar to the teachings of Sherem, Nehor, and Korihor.
6. What sort of things must parents do if they wish their children to grow up as Christians instead of humanists?

Family Teaching Was a Major Part of the Life of Faithful Israelites • FT •

A significant difference between Babylon, the city of the devil, and Zion, the city of God, is in the way they approach the responsibility to teach the children. In Zion, education will be the responsibility of parents and the Church. The ancient Israelites were expected to teach their sons and daughters everything possible or available to know God and man and the universe around them. Besides that, each boy was to be taught a trade or means of making a living, and every girl was to be taught all those things upon which the preservation of life and society and home are dependent. The teaching of a trade was usually the father's direct duty, and trades tended to be passed down from father to son. The wealthy often hired tutors for their children or sent them to a local school taught by available masters.

A careful study of the Book of Mormon will show that the responsibility for supporting and promoting education among the Nephites was in the home and that it remained in the home.

Take-off Passage

Enos 1:1–3.

Other Passages

1 Nephi 1; 2 Nephi 2; Mosiah 1:1–8; Alma 5:6–14; 36–42 (especially 36:17); Helaman 5:5–13; Moroni 8:1; Moses 6:58–62; Proverbs 1:8. (Consider also the education and young life of Jesus, "the carpenter's son," and the education in law and tent-making of Paul. Both of these examples followed the Hebrew pattern.)

Study Questions

1. Learn to recite the stories of faithful Nephite fathers revealed in the above passages. How did they follow the example the Lord taught Adam?
2. How do books of remembrance (journals) enter into or serve in family education?
3. Can a father or mother safely farm out all the education of their children? Which subjects can be most safely farmed out? Which least safely?
4. Why must we not fully rely on the Sunday School, the Primary, and the seminary system for the spiritual education of our children? What precautions should we take?
5. List some of the things the Church has done to help us teach our children in the home. Why is this a proper function of the Church?
6. How are spiritual subjects made to depend upon secular subjects?
7. How do secular subjects depend upon spiritual subjects? In other words, how can we go astray if we learn secular subjects without the control of spiritual subjects?
8. Why do most people overemphasize secular subjects to the dangerous neglect of spiritual subjects?
9. Why is the education of our children one of the greatest responsibilities we have?

The Importance of Scripture Study Was Emphasized by the Nephite Prophets • ISS •

Beginning with those two great brothers, Nephi and Jacob, the Book of Mormon prophets taught by precept and example that the study of holy writ is necessary to man's salvation. King Benjamin admonished his sons to search the scriptures diligently or they would suffer in ignorance. Indeed, a whole people could dwindle and perish in unbelief without the availability of the scriptures. Rather than have this happen to the Nephites, the Lord commanded Nephi to slay Laban to secure the brass plates. Later the Mulekites lost both their knowledge of God's true religion and their language because they came to America without scriptures. (Omni 1:15–17.)

Book of Mormon missionaries and all the faithful searched the scriptures to know the word of God. The scriptures were laid before the Lamanites to bring them to Christ. The making and preservation of the scriptures has been, from the beginning, under the personal care and supervision of our almighty and omniscient Lord himself so that they could be with us now to bless our lives by individual study. It is a great affront to Deity to ignore and neglect them. To ignore and neglect them is as much as to say that we care neither whether God speaks nor what he says. And it is an interesting fact that, as a rule, those who read them the most believe them the most. This is true even of the Bible in the non-LDS world.

Take-off Passage

Mosiah 1:1–8.

Other Passages

1 Nephi 8:24; 2 Nephi 3:12; 4:15; 29:3, 11–13; Alma 17:1–3; 22:12; 37:1–8; 3 Nephi 17:3; 23; 26:1–12; Deuteronomy 31:1–12; Isaiah 8:20; Joseph Smith 2:11; Doctrine and Covenants 42:14; 88:77–80, 118.

Study Questions

1. Why would the Lord expect a mother and housewife to be a student of the scriptures when so much is already required of her?

What other busy people would lose the true and clear vision of their work if they didn't study the scriptures constantly?

2. Why would Joseph Smith say that "a man will get nearer to God by abiding by [the Book of Mormon's] precepts than by any other book?" (Joseph Smith, *History of the Church,* 4:461.)

3. Give some reasons and examples to show that we need to relate all the standard works to each other as we study them.

4. Why should the Book of Mormon be emphasized more than the Bible in our personal early study of the scriptures? When should we begin to give the Bible more of our time? Should we ever neglect it?

5. Why is the Book of Mormon so valuable in missionary work?

6. What advantages would we receive from daily scriptural study? What have the prophets said about this?

The Proper Spirit of Service Is to Remember Always That We Are Serving God • SOS •

King Benjamin taught that public servants, religious or secular, should always remember that they are in the service of their God. And they are *servants,* not masters. It is a Christian duty to serve God. We are not even the masters or owners of our own bodies. They are temples of God and should be kept clean and holy. He has "loaned" them to us. We eventually will be given them forever by the power of the resurrection. But the quality or glory of each person's body then will be determined by what he or she did with it during this life. Hence we are mistaken and even somewhat blasphemous when we say that we can do as we please with our own bodies.

We have become a very self-centered and self-serving people. Even some of the Saints talk of their callings as opportunities to grow and develop instead of opportunities to serve God—usually by serving our fellow men and women. Missionaries sometimes go into the field with the idea that it is a chance to travel, learn a language, or otherwise serve their own selfish ambitions or interests. True, Church service results in growth—if done to serve God. If it is not done to serve God, the chances are that the "growth" will be a snare and a delusion.

And we have no claim for a reward when we serve, according to Benjamin. Of course, a reward comes in a roundabout way. In fact, we are rewarded overmuch constantly, Benjamin says. In addition to everything else, God's grace provides a redemption that we can neither earn nor merit, no matter how great our service. There is a formula, of course, by which we can obtain this salvation; but all our good works and service will not guarantee it. In fact, the good works and good service are an outgrowth of the new creature who is created by a spiritual rebirth.

Take-off Passage

Mosiah 2:17.

Other Passages

Jacob 2:17–19; Mosiah 2:9–27; 4:21; 23:10–12; Helaman 12:1–6; 3 Nephi 24:5; 4 Nephi 23; Matthew 20:20–28. (Note also the story, in Mosiah 28, of Alma the Younger and the sons of Mosiah, who desired to spend their lives in service. Mosiah I, Mosiah II, and other Nephite leaders also devoted their lives to the service of their fellowmen.)

Study Questions

1. Why are laws wrong that diminish our freedom to give our time, talents, and means voluntarily in the true spirit of service?
2. Why is it clear that King Benjamin did not set up a government welfare program supported by taxes?
3. What would have been wrong with his doing so? Would it be any less wrong to force men to give their knowledge away than to give their material wealth away? Why do such systems fail? (See Doctrine and Covenants 134:2.)
4. Why does God's plan leave men free to be saved or damned by how they use or misuse their material and intellectual wealth?
5. Why did Satan promise to save everyone?
6. Why is it impossible to get out of the Lord's debt?
7. Explain in your own words the circumstances under which pursuit of a career or of money in business or government would be safe for your soul.

The Nature of Fallen Man Is Neither Depravity Nor Natural Goodness

• NFM •

There are various views of the nature of man. Some consider him utterly depraved. Others believe that he is basically good and would always turn out lovely and righteous if his "natural" tendencies were allowed to develop properly. Still others think of him as a dual personality: he has one side—the flesh—which is evil, and another side—the spirit—which is good. Among these latter are some who think man can control the flesh and others who excuse man for sinning, blaming sin on the uncontrollable weakness of the flesh. In LDS theology, which is based on revelation, the flesh or physical body has no life or will of itself separate from the life and will of the spirit within. The problem arises when the spirit is placed in a body which is separated from God by that spiritual death which Adam brought upon us, identified in scripture as the fall of man. In this body one experiences temptations which he never had before. In the case of a child, the spiritual death is negated by the Atonement. But when one reaches the age of accountability, he is capable of sinning if he has been taught the law. The effect of this sin is to confirm the spiritual death upon him so that he cannot come back into the presence of God and be happy there unless he obeys the gospel. It is this fallen or carnal man of sin who is "an enemy to God." (Mosiah 3:19.) To regain God's presence he must put off the enmity of the flesh by the exercise of his will unto repentance in Christ with the help of the Spirit of the Lord. In short, he must be spiritually begotten of God and become a new creature.

Take-off Passage

Mosiah 3:19.

Other Passages

1 Nephi 10:6; Mosiah 16:3–5; 27:25; Alma 10:4–6; 30:25; 34:9; 41:11–13; 42:6–10; Helaman 12:1–7; Moses 6:48, 49, 54–62; Doctrine and Covenants 20:11–20; 29:39–48.

Study Questions

1. Explain the relationships that exist between the following scriptural expressions: the natural man; born again; change of heart; new creature; redeemed of the Lord; atonement of Christ.
2. What is the difference between trying to overcome the natural man by external compulsion and doing so by the internal restraint which follows a change of heart?
3. Tell the story of some scriptural characters who overcame the natural man and how they did it.
4. Why is it wrong to say that man is naturally good?
5. Why is it wrong to say that man is utterly depraved?
6. What is wrong with the concept that children suffer from "original guilt"? What relationship does this have to infant baptism?

The Christian and Humanist Opinions of Psychological Disorientation Are Different

• PSYC •

On several occasions the Nephite prophets and missionaries were accused of being "mad" or "deranged." Abinadi was one of these. And he was, of course, out of harmony with the society of King Noah. Being out of harmony or at odds with the world around us is considered a sign of maladjustment or mental sickness in our modern society, as it was in Abinadi's day. But the truth of that accusation depends on the condition of the world we live in. If the world is spiritually and mentally sick, being in harmony with it is sickness.

From a Christian point of view, sin is sickness. We learn from the Bible that homosexuality, which is not only rampant today but is officially tolerated, is one of the prime evidences that a society may be too sick to be saved. Such societies are "ripened in iniquity" and the judgments of God are about to come down upon them and destroy them. As we watch this condition develop, we can see that the judgments often are natural and inevitable. Who can honestly deny that sexual chastity, if universally observed, would not stop many plagues, save millions of lives, and end untold human misery?

It would have been sickness for Abinadi to be in harmony with King Noah and his people or for Lehi to be well adjusted to the political and social mess of 600 B.C. Jerusalem. Remember that the Jews howled against Jeremiah and the other prophets at that time. They could not see any cause for Jeremiah's criticisms and warnings. But every dire prediction was fulfilled, including cannibalism. And it was all a natural consequence of being out of harmony with true reality, the reality of God's law.

Even death is better than surrender to some things. Many times we have to choose between social acceptance and personal honor. What price are you willing to pay to keep your integrity? How cheaply can you be bought in a market that sells prestige, social acceptance, advancement, and worldly honors? The purpose of the gospel is not to help us adjust to the carnal world. We must live in the world, but we must not be of it. The purpose of the gospel is to help us adjust to eternal life.

Everyone who fully accepts Christ is bound to be out of step with his generation except in those choice times when the entire society is converted. The world will judge the Christians as mad; but it is the world which has "gone crazy."

Most people accept the fact that there are people who are irrational for reasons other than sin. We have no quarrel with that. The trouble is that many fail to see that sin is irrational and that it can lead to all sorts of social, political, economic, and spiritual problems. Indeed, most of the ills of humanity could be cured by honest repentance.

Take-off Passage

Mosiah 13:4.

Other Passages

1 Nephi 1:19, 20; 16:1–3; 2 Nephi 8:7; Mosiah 17; Alma 1:3, 7–9; 24:22; 30:16; 60:13, 25–28; Helaman 13:2–5; Luke 6:22, 26; John 5:44; 7:7; 12:43; 15:19; Romans 12:1–3; 1 John 2:15–17; Doctrine and Covenants 1:14–18; 84:49–53.

Study Questions

1. To what situations in your own life can you apply the concept described in PSYC?

2. How is the problem of psychological sickness related to the moral imperative? (See MID.)

3. What is the Book of Mormon prescription for the cure and prevention of psychological sickness, as it is defined in this section?

4. How do welfare/socialist states prevent full and healthy maturation of personality and character?

5. Why is it more natural for women than for men to seek security?

6. Why do men tend to become violent and aggressive towards women when the roles of the sexes become confused? How does this show the wisdom of God's laws that govern homes and families?

7. How do wars and plagues illustrate the natural consequence of the kind of insanity which rejects the laws of our Heavenly Father?

There Can Be No Peace Without Peace in Christ

• PEACE •

The man of the world (natural or fallen man) vainly hopes for peace at a compromise price. He puts his trust in treaties, armies, and summit talks. But the man of God knows there will be no peace in the world until all men are reconciled to Christ and have peace in themselves. For peace proceeds outward from the hearts of men. The world cannot impose it upon mankind by the power of government, and money cannot buy it.

The man of the world builds a United Nations; but the man of God looks "for a city which hath foundations, whose builder and maker is God." (Hebrews 11:10.) There was peace in Enoch's Zion, in Melchizedek's Salem, and among the three generations of Nephites who followed Christ's visit to America; and there will be peace in the Millennium. But we cannot coexist with Satan. To have peace we must cast him out of our hearts, out of our homes, and out of our nations.

Take-off Passage

Mosiah 15:10–18.

Other Passages

1 Nephi 13:37; 14:7; 20:22; 2 Nephi 3:12; 4:27; 19:6, 7; Mosiah 2:28; 4:1–3; Alma 38:8, 15; Helaman 5:44–47; 3 Nephi 12:9; John 14:27; Philippians 4:7; Colossians 3:15; Moses 4:1, 2; Doctrine and Covenants 6:23; 19:23.

Study Questions

1. From Abinadi's point of view, who would be the only peacemakers?
2. How does the atonement of Christ relate to peace?
3. How does the Book of Mormon relate freedom, national peace, and the title of Christ?
4. Under what conditions does the Book of Mormon hold out hope for national or international peace?
5. In what ways and under what circumstances can a person have peace in these times in spite of what is going on in the world?
6. What are the only terms under which you can have peace in Christ?

Without a Legal and Proper Baptism We Cannot Partake of the Atonement • B •

Comparatively few Christians believe any more in the necessity and efficacy of baptism by immersion for the remission of sins. In fact, they hardly ever even consider it a subject worthy of discussion. Some ministers will administer baptism by immersion if requested, though they would usually rather sprinkle if they must do something.

One of the advantages of having a testimony of the truth of the Book of Mormon is that it settles the baptism issue forever. It assures us of the necessity of baptism. It tells us exactly how it is to be done. It tells us exactly why it is to be done and what obligation it places upon us. And it explains the necessity of having divine authority to do it.

Take-off Passage

Mosiah 18:8–16.

Other Passages

2 Nephi 31:5–17; 3 Nephi 11:21–28; Moroni 8; Doctrine and Covenants 22.

Study Questions

1. What questions about baptism does the Book of Mormon settle that the Bible apparently could not settle?
2. What connection is there between baptism and the Savior's commandment to "enter in by the strait gate"? Why "strait" instead of "straight"?
3. How can you use the Book of Mormon to convince people they must be baptized? by immersion?
4. List the obligations to your fellowmen that you take upon yourself when you are baptized.
5. List the obligations to your God that you take upon yourself when you are baptized. What obligation does the Lord take upon himself when you are baptized?
6. What advantages do you hope to gain by a proper baptism?

The Book of Mormon Doctrine of Liberty Is That No People Can Be Free Unless They Worship Christ

• FREE •

The passages presented here are only a small part of those that deal with the subject of liberty; but they are indicative of what may be looked for. All of Alma, from chapter 43 on, as well as some earlier parts, is an account of a war for liberty. Helaman and Third Nephi, in large part, continue this account. This part of the Book of Mormon is not there simply because Mormon was a military man, as some have speculated. It is there because we live in a similar time and need the warning it gives because we are making the same mistakes.

The Book of Mormon shows that sin is the enemy of spiritual and political liberty. No wicked people have ever been free. No wicked people will ever be free. Slavery and freedom, like peace and war, start in the souls of men and women and proceed outward therefrom into the environment. Environment, after all, is only a reflection of the people who make it. Therefore, it is foolishness to suppose that government can create a good environment which, in turn, will make good people.

The Book of Mormon shows that the price of liberty, if it has to be won, is blood—the blood of Christ to purchase our spiritual liberty and the blood of patriots to purchase our physical or political liberty.

If so great a price must be paid for it, how we ought to cherish it and try to preserve it!

When men and women lose their faith and courage, they often look to demagogues who promise what they cannot or should not give. We should remember that we need faith more than bread, and courage more than raiment. When we have faith and courage, we can get the bread and raiment. If government is to give its citizens anything of a material nature, it must first get it from its citizenry. Government doesn't produce anything. Only people produce. Therefore, when people ask the government to solve their economic problems, what they really are saying is, "Take that other man's means away from him and give it to me." Such action is morally wrong. That is why the Lord said that "no government can exist in peace, except such laws are framed and held inviolate as will secure to each individual . . . the right and control of property." (Doctrine and Covenants 134:2.) We only need to look around us to see that violence and civil war result from failure to observe such principles.

The Book of Mormon shows that in general a nation tends to become rich when its citizens are good and free, and that poverty tends to be their lot when they are evil and in bondage. This is because sins tend to reduce productivity and to waste resources. Just consider such a fact as that the grain that is used to produce alcoholic beverages could feed all the hungry of the world. And consider the fact that the price citizens pay for drug control and all other crime control and punishment could take everyone off the poverty rolls. We feed and clothe hundreds of thousands of criminals in our prisons. If the biblical civil code were followed, they would be executed, banished, or forced under threat of death to make restitution; but they would never be imprisoned. There is no scriptural evidence that God condones prisons in peacetime. Only those who have lost faith in the love of God and the reality of life after death think execution of criminals is worse than prison.

The Book of Mormon also shows that God expects us to do our own giving. Charity ceases to be charity when government does our giving for us; because charity is, by definition, voluntary. It was the Gadiantons who promised a share in the spoils if elected. And the amount they shared with their duped followers was probably as small as it is in America today, where less than a third of what we are taxed for the poor ever reaches them. In the times of righteousness, there were no poor among the Nephites because they cared for them out of the goodness of their hearts, not out of the "goodness" of a predatory government.

And again, the Book of Mormon shows that we cannot have good government without good religion; namely, the principles of the gospel of Jesus Christ as revealed in this dispensation. In fact, the Book of Mormon warns us that the United States will go down into spiritual and temporal destruction and slavery if it rejects the Book of Mormon. (1 Nephi 14:6–7.)

Take-off Passage

Mosiah 29.

Other Passages

2 Nephi 5:18; Mosiah 4:16–26; 5:8; Alma 43:29–31; 44:1–7; 46:8–22; 53:17; 58:8–12, 33–41; 60; 61:9, 21; Helaman 14:29–31; John 8:30–36; 2 Corinthians 3:17; Galatians 5; Doctrine and Covenants 56:16, 17; 88:86.

Study Questions

1. Can you cite any examples of times when governments have restored or granted human rights (life, liberty, and the right to own and control property) without the shedding of blood?
2. Discuss the time element involved in losing spiritual and physical liberties.
3. Why would we go unwarned if we were not warned by prophets and other religious leaders? Why can we not rely on politicians to warn us against the loss of our liberty?
4. Why is it impossible to leave your religion (Christian or anti-Christian) behind you when you go into the voting booth?
5. What does the Book of Mormon call a wise vote? an unwise vote? What is the consequence when the majority vote unwisely?
6. Why should people be allowed to vote even if they vote away their freedom?
7. How do both the righteous and the wicked profit when justice catches up with unwise uses of the franchise?

Mosiah Set Up a Christian Constitutional Republic • CCR •

During the American Constitutional Convention, Dr. Benjamin Rush, quoting a Swiss gentleman, said that "Democracy is the devil's own government." When the United States Constitution was written, Benjamin Franklin is supposed to have said, "We have given you a republic; let's see if you can keep it," or words to that effect. There was, in those days, a great distinction made between democracy and republicanism. Our school children were taught this distinction right up until around the turn of the century, when the influence of John Dewey totally permeated American public education. Dewey's philosophy was based on the enthronement of democracy. He believed that all truth—social and scientific—was to be determined by a consensus. Now Americans are very confused about the entire subject.

You can understand the nature of a true Christian constitutional republic when you understand the government of "three whiches" that Mosiah gave to the Nephites. (Mosiah 29:25.) This was a government of laws (1) which were given to their fathers, (2) which were pronounced correct, and (3) which were given to them by God. In a democracy, the voice of the people is sovereign (all-powerful), while in a true Christian constitutional republic, God is sovereign. His sovereignty is expressed mostly through his law.

The colonists were not inclined to accept the Constitution. They were mostly Protestant, and the English influence was very strong. They were steeped in the tradition of the Magna Carta and the Bill of Rights. This philosophy is based on the idea that the government (king) is sovereign and it (he) grants rights to the people. The Constitution was framed on the assumption that God is sovereign, but he grants sovereignty to the people collectively. Therefore, the government has only such rights as the people grant it. This is exactly the opposite of the English tradition. According to R.J. Rushdoony in his book, *This Independent Republic,* a major reason why the colonists finally ratified the Constitution was that the Protestant clergy stumped for it on the grounds that it was based on biblical law, God's law. However, it was also necessary to add a bill of rights to get the approval of the colonists. This was done in the form of amendments so that the basic philosophy of the Constitution could be preserved.

There is no universally accepted definition of what constitutes a republic or what differences exist between democracy and republicanism. However, among many Christians who honor the Constitution, there is some consensus. This consensus embraces two principles: (1) the sovereignty of God and (2) a limited franchise. And these two principles are essentially the basic principles of the Nephite rule of the judges set up by King Mosiah. This is the reason why some people call the Nephite rule of judges a Christian constitutional republic.

The sovereignty of God is easier to discern in the Nephite republic than in the American republic. In fact, the citizens of the American republic for all practical purposes have abandoned the idea of God's sovereignty. It is only to the extent that we are still governed by the Constitution that we recognize God's sovereignty. And even then it is not a conscious recognition of sovereignty, because few recognize or believe that the Constitution was based on biblical law. In the early days of this republic the Bible was the law book of last resort. That is, when judges determined the disposition of cases, they were influenced directly or indirectly by the Bible. They were influenced by the Bible even when they didn't consciously know it. Now they are influenced by the consensus of the legal community as the "law book" of last resort, and few judges allow biblical law to influence their decisions. In other words, we have deteriorated into a democracy, and the people are sovereign in every aspect of our lives. Even our moral values are determined by consensus.

We must always remember that, if God does not rule, men rule. If God's law is abandoned, the laws of men will be embraced. There were cases of the corruption of God's law among the Nephites, too. Those were the times of great trial and trouble. When the prophets are despised, the people suffer poverty, pain, and slavery.

The second principle mentioned above, a limited franchise, is easily misunderstood. The thing to remember is that the franchise need not be limited as to *who* can vote—any reasonable and fair set of voting qualifications will do. But it must be limited as to *what* people can vote on.

In what way, then, should the franchise be limited? As to what you can vote on. Freedom and a true republic cannot be preserved if people can vote to repeal God's law. And they must not vote on whether or not to repeal physical, chemical, economic, or social laws. Bills have been introduced into state legislatures to change pi from 3.1416 . . . to 3.0. It was argued that this would simplify geometry for engineers and others and would make the teaching and learning of mathematics much easier. The Utah legislature once passed a law against the Great Salt Lake being allowed to rise above a certain level. Of course, these lawmakers weren't doing anything as inane as those who tried to change pi. But they might as well have; for it did no good to pass the law. The lake hasn't obeyed that law and neither has the governor. In the meantime, if you will think about it, you will see that our federal government has passed myriad laws which attempt to repeal every known law of economics. And these don't work either. All these laws do is complicate commerce and increase the poverty they are supposed to stop.

The only legitimate use of the franchise is to vote on whether Smith or Jones shall hold political office. And the main standard by which we should judge their worthiness is how we perceive they will defend, support, and execute the constitutional law. Politically speaking, the only good politician is the one who is absolutely knowledgeable about the Constitution and will absolutely defend it. That is why God repeatedly called David the best king. He was on one occasion a murderer and an adulterer in his private life; but he honored the law in his public life. So far as we can tell, David did not tax the people; he did not create a bureaucracy; he absolutely protected the property rights of the people and brought criminals to justice. At least, he did those things better than any other king the Israelites ever had in the Old World. There were better kings in America among the Nephites, but none better in the Old World among the Israelites there.

Of course, the rule of the judges was attacked by the kingmen right from the start. The kingmen were the totalitarians of that day. The totalitarians of our day are (1) the advocates of unlimited democracy (the totalitarianism of the majority which dethrones God), (2) socialists of several varieties, (3) Communists, and (4) Fascists. There are always totalitarians. Maintaining freedom is a constant struggle unless the Lord sets up a special circumstance, as he will during the Millennium. Totalitarianism is the devil's system, and he is always at war against freedom and Christianity.

Take-off Passage

Mosiah 29:11–39.

Other Passages

Alma 10:17, 18, 27; 51; 60; Helaman 6:37–39; 7:5; 3 Nephi 7:6; Luke 11:52; Doctrine and Covenants 98:4–12; 101:77–80, 134. (Study Ezra Taft Benson's speech "The Proper Role of Government," in *An Enemy Hath Done This,* Jerreld L. Newquist, comp. [Salt Lake City: Parliament Publishers, 1969], pp. 125–48.)

Study Questions

1. How has the Lord, in our day, reaffirmed and clarified the law

that he gave to our ancient fathers? Relate this to the "three whiches."

2. Why do the Latter-day Saints have a special reason to accept the United States Constitution?

3. In what practical and limited way is the voice of the people sovereign in a Christian constitutional republic?

4. How is the franchise misused in the United States from a constitutional point of view? How does this make us an unlimited democracy?

5. What is there about the nature of man that makes unlimited democracy dangerous?

6. Why is it impossible for a people to remain free if they have the power to vote themselves or others money from the public treasury?

7. Discuss the difference between the Soviet Socialist Republics and the rule of the Nephite judges with reference to the franchise and sovereignty.

8. How much power must a government have if it is going to redistribute the wealth of its people?

Unrepentant Fallen Man Is Bound by the Chains of Hell • CHH •

There are five punishments for sin: (1) remorse of conscience; (2) natural consequences that follow sins, as a fall follows stepping off a high place; (3) hell, or bondage to the devil; (4) God's or eternal punishment—that great agony suffered on the judgment day if we are not raised with celestial bodies; and (5) the second death, or the final state of the sons of perdition. We can altogether escape from the last three of these punishments by obedience to the gospel. However, the first two are, to some extent, a condition of this life that we must suffer as long as we are here.

Hell is that condition of the body, mind, and soul we are in when we have chosen to obey Satan rather than God. In this life happiness and hell exist side by side. In the postmortal spirit world there is a greater separation, and hell becomes more literally a place as well as a condition. After the resurrection, Satan and all those who belong to him will go away into perdition, which is a completely separated place without glory that is sometimes referred to also as hell. To be in hell is to be bound by Satan's chains. We make ourselves his servents by rebelling against God.

Take-off Passage

Alma 12:11–17.

Other Passages

2 Nephi 1:13, 23; 9:12, 45, 46; 28:19–23; Alma 34:34; 36:18; Romans 6:16; Moses 7:26.

Study Questions

1. Name three circumstances or times in which a person can successively be bound by the chains of hell or be said to be in hell.
2. How does one escape the chains of hell according to the Book of Mormon?
3. What effect do the chains of hell have on one's knowledge?
4. What difference exists between bad habits and good habits which reveals the existence of a real, coercive power of evil?
5. Is there really such a thing as a good habit in the sense of a compulsive urge that is hard to resist?
6. What is the difference in effect upon you and upon your agency in obeying a good man and obeying an evil man?

The Foreknowledge of God Is Infinite • FG •

Hardly anything is more clearly revealed in the scriptures than the fact that God has an infinite foreknowledge. In addition to outright statements to that effect, every prophecy is proof of that infinite foreknowledge. Yet some have come up with the rational agreement that if God had an infinite foreknowledge, we wouldn't have free agency: we'd be compelled to do whatever God knew we were going to do.

Actually free agency is a condition of this life—perhaps all eternity—that God defends and preserves. No doubt his infinite foreknowledge gives him the power and the wisdom to defend and preserve it. In fact, fulfillment of prophecy would require interference with our free agency if God did *not* have an infinite foreknowledge. If the past, future, and present are all present with him (Doctrine and Covenants 38:2), he can *see* the future as immediately as he can see the present. If that were not the case, he would have to *contrive* the future in order to fulfill prophecy. And, if he had to contrive the future, we would, indeed, be pawns of predestination.

But we do not need rational arguments to defend the infinite foreknowledge of God. We only need to exercise enough faith to believe that, if God says he has an infinite foreknowledge, it must be so; and if he says men are free, they must be free; and if he says both of these things, they must not conflict with each other. If we have settled, once and for all and absolutely, the question of how we got the Book of Mormon, the rest is easy.

Take-off Passage

Alma 13:7.

Other Passages

1 Nephi 9:5; 14:22; 2 Nephi 9:20; 27:10; Words of Mormon 1:7; Mosiah 4:9; Alma 13:3; 37:2, 12, 14, 18; 46:23, 24; Ether 3:25–27; Moses 1:8; Doctrine and Covenants 3:19; 10:1–46; 88:41.

Study Questions

1. What fundamental principles of the gospel are necessary corollaries to or are dependent upon God's foreknowledge?
2. What prophecies and their fulfillment can you cite to demonstrate God's foreknowledge as it applies to nations and individuals?
3. Why would the opinion or conviction that God does not have infinite foreknowledge fail to help you to live better?
4. Why is it impossible to understand the Atonement without accepting the infinite foreknowledge of God?
5. Why are revealed facts superior to rational arguments on the subject of foreknowledge?
6. Explain in your own words why a person never has any more than his own word to back him up when he questions or denies a revealed fact. (See Alma 30:40.)

It Is Our Privilege to Be Instruments in the Hands of God • IHG •

In the previous topic (FG), we raised the question of free agency's compatibility with God's infinite foreknowledge. Part of the answer is found in Alma's soliloquy found in Alma 29:1–9. He commences by mourning the fact that he does not have the power of an angel so that he could overwhelm all mankind with the greatness of the gospel and in effect force them to accept salvation. Then he says, "But behold, I am a man, and do sin in my wish." He then proceeds to explain, among other things, that (1) as a general rule, God gives every nation or people the amount of information they want, as demonstrated by what they have done with what they have. (2) Individuals are raised up to give this amount of information in their own tongue to their own nations. (3) We are instruments in the Lord's hands in spreading whatever portion of the word the Lord, in his wisdom, sees as fit, proper, and just for each nation and people. (4) It is to our glory that we can be the instruments of the Lord.

From the above we can infer that the Lord has foreordained certain people to come at certain times so that all the rest of mankind, through these chosen leaders, prophets, and missionaries, will have an adequate chance to exercise their agency and determine their ultimate salvation or damnation. We also can infer that many of the chosen teachers will be left temporarily without a full knowledge of the gospel so that they will teach only what they are supposed to teach. But, if that is the case, it will be made up to them later on. If their intent is to be God's instruments, and if they so conduct their lives, they will receive the reward of an instrument of God.

People are not the only instruments of God in prearranging history so that all mankind can exercise choice. For example, the Book of Mormon is one of the greatest instruments ever devised to bring about the purposes of the Lord. It is the prime instrument of our day to reconcile souls with Christ. The Bible, too, was nurtured down through the ages and designed as a great instrument for people both in and out of the Church. There are some imperfections in it; but they are as nothing compared to the great power it still has to work upon the souls of men and women to bring them to better and greater choices. In the Siberian labor camps, prisoners have been brought to a great conviction of the divinity of Christ and his work by reading just scraps of the Bible—sometimes only those scraps preserved in the writings of Tolstoy, whose works Stalin made the mistake of not destroying.

Besides people and books of scripture, modern inventions, such as television, are instruments in the hands of the Lord to bring the word to all who have ears to hear. Scientific advancement blossomed just before and came to fruition just after the introduction of the present dispensation of the gospel. Many natural explanations for this have been advanced by great thinkers in the Church; but no explanation is better than the simple fact that the Lord so arranged it for his own instrumentality in bringing about his eternal purposes without interfering with the agency of man. Thus scientific geniuses also can be instruments in the Lord's hands—whether or not they intend to be.

Take-off Passage

Alma 29:1–9.

Other Passages

2 Nephi 1:24; 3:24; Mosiah 23:10; 27:36; Alma 1:8; 2:30; 17:11; 26:3; 35:14; Doctrine and Covenants 1:1–5; 42:6; 81:2–5; 84:75–87; 88:77–81.

Study Questions

1. How do missionaries affect the Book of Mormon's instrumentality?
2. How does the Book of Mormon affect and improve the instrumentality of missionaries?
3. What can we learn from the attitude and actions of Book of Mormon prophets and missionaries that will improve us as instruments of the Lord?
4. How does the Book of Mormon work as an instrument in bringing people to Christ? in bringing them to baptism? Why can they not have the one without the other?
5. Relate this subject of instruments to section 20 of the Doctrine and Covenants.

Korihor Exalted Human Reason Above Revelation • KR •

When we call Korihor a rationalist, we are emphasizing a common but oversimplified definition of the term. One accepted idea of what the philosophy of rationalism proposes is that the human intellect is the supreme source of knowledge and truth, that revelation is unnecessary and nonexistent, and that religious truths can be discovered and refined by the human mind alone without inspiration. In that sense, Korihor was a rationalist. But many rationalists would reject that definition. Some, such as James Martineau, the nineteenth-century theologian and rationalist, would even claim that miracles can occur; but they would argue that their meaning must be subject to human reason. Other rationalists would argue that miracles that do not make sense to the human mind must be rejected as spurious. That is, they insist on a "reasonable or rational world," as they see the world. Korihor argued that it was not reasonable to believe in Christ or in prophecy. "No man can know that which is to come." This is a quite common, though not universal, rationalist position.

Treatises on rationalism very commonly point out that rationalism arose as an alternative to "revelationism" or the literal reliance upon and interpretation of scripture. So religious people who attack rationalism do so out of the belief that rationalism is the enemy of revelation. And, of course, radical rationalism always has been the enemy of revelation and the prophets, just as Korihor was the enemy of revelation and the prophets.

In this section we are using Korihor as the prototype of all that is evil in rationalism. In that sense rationalism is, to a great extent, one of the parents of such other evils as behaviorism, organic evolution, relativism, humanism, socialism, and so on. Neither rationalism nor these other "evils" are necessarily totally evil. All of them have advanced human knowledge; and therefore they are useful even if in no other way than the way in which Satan serves a purpose in this life—that is, as the "opposition" in all things. (2 Nephi 2:15.) If he didn't serve a purpose here, the Lord never would have temporarily banished him here instead of sending him straight to perdition, wherever that is. (Of course, Satan is totally evil, while the above relatives of rationalism are not.)

There is nothing in "Mormonism" which is anti-rational in an ultimate sense. It is just that we realize that only God, the infinite being, is capable of defining what is rational and what is irrational. Our minds are always afflicted with ignorance and error. Hence there are gaps which we cannot fill—gaps which cause us to be irrational to a greater or lesser degree.

Once we have understood this weakness of humanity—this propensity for ignorance and error—and have received a divine testimony of the truth of the Book of Mormon, we can reason in the following way: We know that the scriptures are true, except for possible errors in the Bible—which is a very minor problem. Therefore, our job is to use our reasoning powers to determine *what they say* not to *sit in judgment on their truth.* We do not read Nephi and Isaiah and ask ourselves if they were right or wrong. We read them and ask ourselves what they say. We use to its limit every gray cell we possess, to decipher the meaning; but we do not use one ounce of mental energy trying to decide whether Isaiah and Nephi were repeating only the superstitions of their times. We already got that problem out of the way when we made that great discovery by personal revelation that the Book of Mormon is true.

Of course, this process of "reasoning" out the meaning of the scriptures is a rational process. Therefore we too are rationalists in a sense. But we are a different kind of rationalist from Korihor and all those people who think the scriptures must be judged by the current knowledge consensus of the learned world.

A poor, confused rationalist (of the Korihor type), on the other hand, has never paid the price of a testimony of the truth of the Book of Mormon. So he doesn't know about any of the standard works. He is in the pitiful and impossible position of having to forever compare their words with the words of his truly cherished authorities, the scientists and humanists, to determine what he will believe and what he will reject. After all, that is all he does when he uses what he fondly calls his "reasonable mind." Reasoning or rationalism is never more than running the new idea past all the old ideas stored in the "computer" we call a mind. And if there is any ignorance or error there, the output will be adversely affected.

That doesn't mean that the faithful will never make mistakes about what the prophets said. But if they keep forever at the task of reading and trying to understand the scriptures, they will be following a safe course. They know that because they know that the Book of Mormon is true and that it came the way Joseph Smith said it came.

It is important to remember that Alma made Korihor stick to his original premises; and then he showed him that, of necessity these premises made Korihor's whole case rest on his "word only." (Alma 30:37–43.) Alma, on the other hand, had much for Korihor to consider and weigh in studied judgment: (1) "the testimony of all these thy brethren"; (2) the testimony of "all the holy prophets"; (3) "the scriptures"; and (4) "all things." (Alma 30:44.)

Take-off Passage

Alma 30.

Other Passages

2 Nephi 2:18–27; 9:27, 28, 42, 43; 28:6; Jacob 4:8; 7:2–7; Alma 1:2–5; Helaman 16:17–20; 1 Corinthians 2; Doctrine and Covenants 50:1–24.

Study Questions

1. What relationships do you see between this section and RVHK?
2. How can it be shown that organic evolution rests entirely upon rationalism or the reasoning of human minds—not on empiricism, properly defined, nor on revelation?
3. What basic tenets do you see in education and the social sciences that are derivatives from or are corollaries of organic evolution?
4. Identify some teachings of the carnal mind that Korihor taught in order to have success. (Alma 30:53.)
5. In what ways is rationalism, as here defined, pleasing to the carnal mind?
6. Identify some areas today in which men are having success because they teach Korihor's concepts.
7. How do today's "get rich quick" and "success" books relate to Korihor and his philosophy?

The Word Is More Powerful Than the Sword

• WORD •

It was a time of crisis in the Church and in the nation. There were indications that the apostate Zoramites were about to join forces with the Lamanites and stir them up to war against the Nephites. This meant the threat of a massive invasion bringing death and destruction from a savage, relentless enemy determined to avenge imagined wrongs. It is not difficult to visualize oneself in the situation that Alma and the other Nephite prophets and patriots faced.

In these circumstances, Alma remembered that no wars are won with swords unless they also are won with ideas. Ideas do, after all, have consequences. In fact, all actions proceed forth out of the idea matrix. People usually act to increase a sense of well-being or to decrease a sense of discomfort. And they generally do what they believe will improve their lot. Alma knew that Christ is the Father of peace and Satan is the father of war. So he decided to "try the virtue of the word of God." (Alma 31:5.)

This lesson can be applied to the operation of families, wards, and stakes. We always have a tendency to think that, if we can compel people by social pressure or other means to mimic the life of a Saint, our work will have been done. But we have it turned around. We need to see that works are the consequence of conversion, not the reverse. If we get that through our heads we will not be forever trying to improve the statistics. We will instead commence trying to help people obtain the improvement of true conversion. After that conversion the statistics will take care of themselves and will become what they were intended—just a part of the historical record that the Lord requires. They can, of course, be used as a barometer to tell us how well we are doing in the conversion business; but then there always will be the temptation to misuse them.

No contest, competition, or outwardly imposed stimulus can match the inner motivation of a regenerated Saint. There is no shortcut, no substitute. Each person must be born again. He cannot have this rebirth of the Spirit until he knows *why* he must and *how* he can. He has to receive this information by the oral or written word. For every one who can be reached by the written word, there are dozens who respond more quickly—at least, at first—to the oral word. If it is done by the power of the Spirit, which carries it into the hearts of men, there is no substitute for the preaching of the word. We can improve the efficiency and clarity of presentation, but we cannot do without it. We can do nothing to improve statistics that will work as well as "bearing down in pure testimony" in preaching the word. The greatest thing we can do is bring souls to Christ. It is doubtful that anything has motivated so many to become teachers and missionaries as the scriptures and stories in this part of the Book of Mormon. (See ISS.)

Take-off Passage

Alma 31:5.

Other Passages

2 Nephi 25:24–30; Jacob 4:4, 5, 14; Jarom 1:11; Mosiah 3:14, 15; 12:31, 37; 13:27–35; 16:14, 15; Alma 25:15, 16; 30:3; 3 Nephi 1:24, 25; 9:17; 12:17–19; 15:2–10; Romans 11:25; Galatians 3:24; Hebrews 11:40.

Study Questions

1. What connections do you see between this section and the one called HG?
2. What scriptural incidents or stories can you cite that demonstrate the power of the word?
3. Explain what *word* means as used in this section.
4. Explain how the power of the word is the secret of the success of the missionary discussions of the Church.
5. Show how this principle (WORD) is the foundation of all the programs of the Church as they come out from the General Authorities. If they are corrupted thereafter, what is the reason?
6. If you were a bishop or stake president, how could you use this principle to improve statistics within the framework of the Church programs? Describe, for example, how you would go about increasing fast offerings.

The Way to Life Is Through the "Great Plan of the Eternal God" • GP •

Brigham Young very often reminded the Saints that the reason they did not give their whole souls to God was that they were afraid he might interfere with their plans. He might "take their wives or their little ones" or remove their wealth. One of his sermons on the subject inspired the following verse entitled, "I Trust You, Lord—Almost:"

Oh, Father of all! Oh, Lord divine!
I'll answer your call; but don't touch mine!
Don't take my wife; spare my child;
don't touch my life, or the goods I've piled.
I'll do anything you want me to:
to you I'll bring what's just and due.
But keep me rich; don't change my fate;
don't empty my dish or make bare my plate.
I trust you, Lord—but there's a limit.
So give me your word you'll stay within it.

Relative to planning lives there is a persistent and strident voice in the land telling girls and women that they own their own bodies and can do anything they wish with them—even to conceiving unwanted children and then terminating their lives in the womb. We have been told until nearly all of us believe it that it is proper for the government to solve our economic and social problems by taking one man's property and giving it to another. This is the great plan of coercion that was foreshadowed in the plan Satan presented in the councils of heaven.

These days we talk a lot about planning. Everybody has a plan. We have plans to build homes, plans to make dresses, plans for the day, plans for parties, plans for what we are going to do with our lives.

Do you trust yourself to make a plan for your life and your family? Would you not feel better, safer, and more assured if you were following "the great plan of the Eternal God?" (Alma 34:9.)

The Lord has revealed that he has a plan for you and for all of his children. It is a plan of deliverance, redemption, mercy, salvation and happiness. It is a plan or road map to bring us back to his presence forever. The Book of Mormon reveals this plan to us for our living today. It is not just a way or a plan, but the only plan we can trust and live to bring us into his presence again.

Take-off Passage

Alma 34:9.

Other Passages

2 Nephi 9:6; 13:28; Alma 12:25; 12:30; 13:1–6; 24:14; 34:16; 41:2; 42:8; 42:15; 3 Nephi 26:4–5; Doctrine and Covenants 3:1; Moses 4:1–4; 6:62; Abraham 3:17–28; 4:21; 1 Peter 1:20.

Study Questions

1. What does the Book of Mormon say about changing the Lord's plan? (See Alma 12:26.)
2. Why is it wrong to say we own our own bodies and can do as we please with them? What does belief in organic evolution have to do with this? What does belief in the concept of premortal covenants have to do with it?
3. Identify some teachings and life-styles that are contrary to "the great plan of the Eternal God."
4. What does it take to know and understand the plan of God for a way of life?
5. Are there any major steps or decisions in your life now that the Lord's plan should help you make?

The Meaning of the Law of Moses Is Lost If Its Connection to Christ Is Overlooked

• MLM •

While today's experts on Judaism are very learned in all the details of the feast days, the fast days, the calendars, the minutiae of legal technicalities, and the history of the law of Moses, they rarely know the most essential fact—that the law of Moses had no meaning without Christ. Without faith in Christ and a great understanding of the New Testament commentary on the law of Moses, it would be difficult to find this most important aspect of the law of Moses in the Old Testament. In fact, the meaning of the law of Moses is obscure even in the New Testament. Too many of "the plain and precious things" have been deleted. But the Book of Mormon supplies all of these things which are most precious to a proper understanding of the law of Moses.

Take-off Passage

Alma 34:13–14.

Other Passages

2 Nephi 33:1–5; Jacob 1:19; Enos 1:3; Mosiah 4:1; 28:1–3; Alma 4:19; 11:46; 14:6, 7; 15:3–12; 18:40; 19:9; 20:17–27; 22:17; 23:3; 26:3; 37:9, 10; Ether 12:23–28; Moroni 6:4; Ezekiel 3:17–19; 1 Corinthians 1:21; 1 Thessalonians 1:5, 6; Doctrine and Covenants 42:11–15; 100:4–8.

Study Questions

1. What principles of the gospel were lost to the followers of Judaism by the end of the dispensation of Christ and his Apostles?
2. How can you show that some of the first principles of the gospel were still a part of the law of Moses in the days of Jesus and John the Baptist?
3. What evidence is there that the power of God left the practitioners of the law of Moses when that law was fulfilled? How does the lack of a temple and prophets figure in this?
4. What fulfilled the law of Moses?
5. How do you know that the "eye for an eye" statements were

a symbolic expression of the ethic of the law of Moses instead of real practices of the legal system?

6. Were the blood offerings peculiar to the law of Moses or were they instituted earlier? If so, by whom? What did blood offerings symbolize?

7. How were the stern punishments and practices of the law a "type" or "shadow" of Christ? (Mosiah 3:15.)

Faith in Christ Is a Great Motivator

• FAITH •

Faith is a gift or quality of character which moves people to good action. It is the opposite of fear and doubt. Faith in God as they perceived him and in themselves caused the Founding Fathers of the United States to establish a free nation in which men and women could let their own resourcefulness and a bounteous nature work together to create the highest living standard any nation has enjoyed as far as we know.

It is not just *faith,* however, but *faith in Christ* that is the first principle of the gospel. Faith in Christ causes us to hope for a better life here and in the world to come. This hope causes us to come down into the depths of humility and experience a broken heart and a contrite spirit and to dedicate our lives to Christ. It causes us to pattern our lives after his life and to keep his commandments.

Take-off Passage

Alma 34:15–17.

Other Passages

Enos 1:5–8; Mosiah 4:1–3; Alma 22:12–18; 32:21–43; 33:19–23; 36:17; 37:33; Helaman 15:7; Ether 12:3–23; Moroni 7:25, 38–43; John 14:12; James 2:14–26; Doctrine and Covenants 20:29.

Study Questions

1. Why is it not enough to just have faith in a good way of life—faith in knowledge, or faith in Buddha, for example? Why must it be faith in Christ?

2. How do Book of Mormon teachings concerning the Atonement and the nature of man tie in with the teaching of faith in Christ? (See NFJ and NFM.)

3. What principles of the gospel were taught by Book of Mormon prophets to build faith within people? Give examples of times when these principles created faith.

4. Why is repentance impossible without faith in Christ? What is it called when a person discards bad habits without faith in Christ?

5. By various examples, demonstrate how faith operates as a motivator to action. How do farmers, for example, demonstrate faith?

6. By Book of Mormon definition, can a person have faith in something evil or erroneous? (See Alma 32:21.)

7. Can a person have faith in socialism or communism or fascism or any other similar belief, according to this Book of Mormon definition? Is there a counterfeit of faith?

Prayers Are Heard and Answered • P •

Some think that prayer is only communion of self with better self. They think there is little or no hope of an answer except as things tend to fall into better perspective when a person communes with himself or herself in the time of worship. The Book of Mormon, however, teaches a real communication with a God who not only can hear us all but also does hear us all and will answer when we ask in faith.

Take-off Passage

Alma 34:18–27.

Other Passages

2 Nephi 32:4, 8, 9; Enos 1:1–8; Mosiah 26:13, 14; 27:14; Alma 22:18; 34:38; 37:36, 37; 38:13, 14; 3 Nephi 18:18–23; Ether 2:14, 15; Matthew 21:21, 22; John 14:13, 14; James 1:5–7.

Study Questions

1. List ten scriptural cases of literal (real) answers to prayers involving both temporal and spiritual matters.

2. Do the scriptures warrant the use of prayer for the improvement of one's economic circumstances? What is the connection between temporal and spiritual affairs? How does this expose the fallacy in the idea that "human rights" are more important than "property rights"?

3. How are Book of Mormon teachings concerning prayer associated with Book of Mormon teachings concerning God's omniscience?

4. What relationship exists between the fast offering, for example, and answers to prayer? Why could the prayers of Cornelius be answered? (Acts 10.)

5. How do you know that a person has rejected the truth of the scriptures when he teaches that prayer's main or only purpose is communion with one's better self?

"Except a Man Be Born Again, He Cannot See the Kingdom of God" • BA •

Some have a certain spiritual awakening which makes it possible for them to "see" the kingdom of God—that is, recognize that the gospel has been restored and the true Church has been reestablished on the earth. Then, if they are "born of the water and of the Spirit," they are able to enter the Church; and, if they endure to the end, they can enter into their rest in God's kingdom.

Some are "stillborn." That is, they do not act upon that first spiritual awakening which gives them the knowledge or intimation of the great thing which has happened. One retired Lutheran minister in Winona, Minnesota, in 1941, who received a testimony of the truth of the Book of Mormon but did not join the Church, asked the Elder who helped him get that far (Glenn Pearson), "How many 'Mormons' are there?"

The Elder replied, "About 750,000."

The minister then said, "Well, if all who know it is true were to be baptized, I suspect you would have 7,500,000 members."

The astonished Elder asked, "Why do you think that?"

The minister said, "I believe that, out of every ten who know that 'Mormonism' is true, only one ever joins the Church."

"Why do they not join?" asked the Elder.

"Mostly, I suppose, because of these things"—and the minister held out a cigar in one hand and a cup of coffee in the other.

But, of course, there are other reasons for so many spiritual stillbirths. The Word of Wisdom may have been the biggest stumbling block on the path to the baptismal font in that day; but it surely isn't now. Among other things, unchastity and the pride of the intellectual mind in the "precepts of men" are greater problems today. In any event, the two major things that keep people out of The Church of Jesus Christ of Latter-day Saints are sin and ignorance.

The sorrows and frustrations of this mortal world are inflicted upon us mostly by wicked men who seem incapable of exercising self-control. The only solution is the one Christ has given us: We must have a change of heart and become new creatures with a new Spirit which will sanctify our souls and give us the power we need to overcome the flesh. Paul recognized—as do all the prophets—that there is a certain amount of war within because of the "enmity of the flesh." But no psychological adjustment is more than a half measure except the one that the Great Physician prescribed. Christ is the Great Physician of human souls. He is the begetter and deliverer in our spiritual rebirth. It is when we see him as he is that the mighty change can be wrought within us.

Take-off Passage

Alma 36:5–26.

Other Passages

Mosiah 5:2–7; 27:23–28; Alma 5:7–25; 7:14; 22:15; 38:6; John 3:3–5; Moses 6:59–61.

Study Questions

1. Why did Alma ask old baptized members of the Church if they had been born of God?
2. What relationship do you see between Book of Mormon teachings on this subject and the so-called motivation to do right and to exercise self-control?
3. How can a person know if he has been born again?
4. How is this principle associated with the atonement of Christ?
5. What three things happen to a convert which justify calling his experience a rebirth?

When We Die We Go into a Spirit World • SW •

Between the death of the mortal body and its resurrection we live in a spirit world. That world, though invisible to our mortal eyes, is near, in, and above this earth. In this spirit world the righteous and the wicked are more completely separated than they are in this life.

There are various names for the places of the wicked and the righteous. In the Bible the place of the righteous was sometimes called Abraham's bosom, and the place of the wicked was called hell, sheol, or hades, depending on the language. Sheol also did service for the whole world of the dead. And paradise, a Greek word, originally meant a "park" or "place of waiting." Hence it could mean simply the whole spirit world. However, by Joseph Smith's day paradise had come to mean heaven or the place of the righteous. In the Book of Mormon the usual names for heaven are heaven or paradise, and the usual name for hell is hell. One has to consult the commentaries of the linguistic experts to be sure of what is meant in the Bible in every case. Even then, whether he gets the correct interpretation will depend on which experts he consults and how well he understands what they say.

If we endure with faith in Christ and repentance to the end of our mortal lives, we go to the spirit world paradise to wait for a joyous resurrection. Of course, we do not just wait. While in this "rest of the Lord," we can be sent on missions to the "prison house," as hell has sometimes been named.

If we do not endure to the end or have never got onto the path, we go to hell or the prison house. There our condition is described as one of misery. Perhaps the misery varies according to the degree of wickedness. After all, the wicked in this life are in misery, too; and they seldom realize it. In any event, Satan has greater and more immediate or personal power over us in hell than in this life. Hell is his present home. Perdition is his future home.

Take-off Passage

Alma 40:6–15.

Other Passages

2 Nephi 9:10–13; 4 Nephi 14; Moroni 10:34; Matthew 14:26; Luke 16:22–25; 24:36–39; 1 Peter 3:18–21; 4:6; Doctrine and

Covenants 138. (See *Teachings of the Prophet Joseph Smith,* comp. Joseph Fielding Smith [Salt Lake City: Deseret Book Co., 1938], pp. 310–57, and Joseph F. Smith, *Gospel Doctrine* [Salt Lake City: Deseret Book Co., 1966], p. 472.)

Study Questions

1. How does Joseph F. Smith's vision of the redemption of the dead clarify the Bible and confirm the Book of Mormon?
2. What passages of scripture or incidents in the scriptures give you a knowledge of what a personage of spirit looks like?
3. What concepts in the Book of Mormon bring peace and happiness to a person who has loved ones in the spirit world?
4. In what way is death a partial judgment?
5. Under what circumstances does work for the dead prove helpful to the spirits in prison?

God Has Bound Himself to Respect the Relationship Between Justice and Mercy • RJM •

Every good and normal person has a sense of justice and mercy. Even the wicked seem to want a just and merciful world, especially in an ultimate or eternal sense. Even in times of great wickedness, the Nephites wanted prophets for commanders of their armies.

Justice and mercy seem to be in opposition to each other: the one seeks a payment for each offense; the other yearns to forgive or to be forgiven. Christ, as the Judge and also the Redeemer of all men, has reconciled these two qualities within himself through his atonement and by offering the law of the gospel as the means by which we can obtain the benefits of his atonement. Having paid the price of all sin himself, he has obtained the legal right to forgive the truly penitent—those who have obeyed the gospel. The good are appreciative of the fact that they can depend upon the justice as well as the mercy of God. The wicked stand in fear of his justice because their sins condemn them. Of course, we all would stand condemned if there were no opportunity to repent made possible by the Atonement.

God is a God of truth. He does not lie. If he lied, he would cease to be God by definition; for God, by universal agreement of the definition of the word *God* and the nature of the being of God, does not lie. He has said that he will not rob justice; therefore, he will not. This means that he can forgive only those sinners who have a claim on his mercy through the Atonement and through their repentance from all of their sins. This does not mean that the Lord is forced by any external power to forgive only repentant sinners. He is only compelled internally by his own honor. He is not dependent on anyone for his power. And he plays no favorites. All are treated equally and equitably. Sin is punished either in Christ (through the Atonement) or in the sinner (by God's or eternal punishment). And obedience is rewarded by escape from punishment or any condition which limits progress and happiness.

Take-off Passage

Alma 42:12–28.

Other Passages

2 Nephi 2:6–10; 9:46; 11:5; Jacob 6:3–13; Mosiah 3:24–27; 15:7–9, 27; Alma 7:12; 10:21; 12:32–34; 34:15–17; 3 Nephi 26:5; Doctrine and Covenants 88:35.

Study Questions

1. What principles of the gospel, by their operation or practice, assure one that justice and mercy will be measured in proper balance?
2. Why do the concepts of justice and mercy lose their meaning and become rhetorical symbols when the concept of the Atonement is forsaken?
3. What relationships are there between Gethsemane, repentance, mercy, and relying on the merits of Christ?
4. What will decrease our fear of justice and increase our assurance of mercy?
5. What does the statement "perfect love casteth out all fear" have to do with justice and mercy?

The Book of Mormon Justifies Wars of Defense • W •

There are very few, if any, issues in the world today that are more divisive than war—to fight or not to fight. Vietnam and Korea are monuments to this divisiveness, for the divided counsels in America caused her to lose both of those wars. And, in the peace, many more were murdered by the victors than died in the military actions when the United States was engaged. At least, that is true for Vietnam.

The Book of Mormon is quite clear about war: (1) it is the result of the wickedness of fallen men in a fallen world; (2) it always is started by the evil designs of power-hungry totalitarians; and (3) good men and good nations should never go to war except to defend their liberty, their lives, their families, and their property. Also, in the case of the Anti-Nephi-Lehies, the Book of Mormon points up some rare conditions under which a Christian would be justified in being a conscientious objector even if his freedom were at stake: he had fought and killed so much—and loved it—before his conversion, that any further killing would jeopardize his eternal salvation. Normally, however, people are expected to defend their lives, families, liberty, and property.

In modern revelation, the Lord has declared that war will be among us until the second coming of Christ. (Doctrine and Covenants 63:32–34.) War will be part of the judgments that will make a full end of all nations. (Doctrine and Covenants 87.) He has commanded us to renounce war and proclaim peace. (Doctrine and Covenants 98:16.) He has given us his law that justifies the Saints in entering into battle. (Doctrine and Covenants 98:23–38.)

A significant number of the pages of the Book of Mormon deal with war. It was written for us and it very likely was intended to advise us on the problems we have with wars, with pacifists or "doves," and with "hawks" or "warmongers." It gives many great teachings on war to guide the Saints in every nation. And they certainly need guidance; for the Lord has said that the Saints "shall hardly escape." (Doctrine and Covenants 63:34.)

Take-off Passage

Alma 43:1–3.

Other Passages

1 Nephi 14:10–14, 22; Alma 43; 3 Nephi 7; Doctrine and Covenants 1:17–19; 63:32–34; 87; 98:16–38. (See PEACE, HATE, ADC, PD, KR, GC, FREE, and Ezra Taft Benson, *God, Family, Country* [Salt Lake City: Deseret Book Co., 1974].)

Study Questions

1. What is the basic cause of war, according to the scriptures?

2. Why do men fight wars over land or property? (See conference talk by President David O. McKay, October 1962.)

3. What does the Book of Mormon teach about victory, the peace conference tables, corruption in government, prisoners of war, draft dodgers, disarmament, men of arms, the price of political freedom, protected sanctuaries, and so on? What does it teach about threatened enemy occupation of other "parts of the land, which would lay a foundation for serious consequences" (Alma 50:32)? How does all this apply to our situation today?

4. What do you believe the Church is doing today to avoid the evils of war? Why can you safely say that the LDS missionary system is the greatest anti-war program in the world?

5. What does it take to justify a Saint in going to war?

6. Compare the Book of Mormon and the American press as sources for a philosophy about war.

Hate Is Generated by Satan • HATE •

The Savior made it clear that, if a person or institution testifies or teaches against the world, the world in return will turn the satanic forces of hate against that person or institution. (John 7:7; 15:18.) Hate is the force all antichrists use to set men and institutions against each other. Evil, designing men can obtain power over people in this way. (Alma 43:7–8.) Hate can motivate people in war. Hate can be taught. (4 Nephi 1:39.) Conspiring men study and develop the technique of teaching and generating hate with zeal and determination just as Christians try to develop true Christian love. (See Eugene Methvin, *Riot Makers* [New Rochelle: Arlington House, 1970].)

Take-off Passage

Alma 43:7–8.

Other Passages

1 Nephi 8:26–28; 22:5; 2 Nephi 8:7; 29:5; Jacob 7:26; Mosiah 10:17; 3 Nephi 3:4; 11:28, 29; 4 Nephi 1:38, 39; Luke 6:22; John 7:7; 15:18; 16:1–4; 1 John 3:13; Doctrine and Covenants 43:21; 124:50.

Study Questions

1. How can this section help you escape the trap of mob or crowd mentality?

2. Show how "raising an issue" can result in damage to the home, the school, or the Church. Why must the "raising of an issue" consist of an attack against some God-given truth if it is to serve the purpose of creating hate? What does this have to do with the Marxist dialectic? Why is the devil always satisfied with a compromise, even if it is a seemingly little one?

3. Give some examples of ways in which men have gained and are gaining power over people by teaching them to hate.

4. Why do the Marxists work so hard at keeping hate towards Hitler alive?

5. Why is it that many apostates hate the LDS Church and its leaders more than any other people? Why is their whole program a hate-the-Mormons program?

6. How did the Lamanites teach their children to hate the Nephites? Who was it who later stirred up hatred against the Nephites?

Freedom and Prosperity Are Based on the Land • L •

A rule of propaganda is that the bigger the falsehood and the more often it is presented the more likely it will be that people will believe it. One of the biggest errors of all time is that "human rights are more important than property rights." Before the 1930s very few Americans believed it. But it was repeated so often during the Great Depression that soon people believed it. Since then few Americans even question it, and even fewer could tell you why it is an error. The reason, of course, is that, if they did not believe this error, the practice of the redistribution of wealth by the power of government could not be justified.

The truth of the matter is that all human rights are based on property rights. And all property rights are based on the land. The history of the struggle for freedom from the feudal lords in the western world is a history of the struggle to break the feudal monopoly on land. Those poor, oppressed people rightly saw that they had no hope unless "their homes, too, were their castles" and they could call a piece of land their own. The struggle to have the right to own land without being a nobleman or a government bureaucrat was won by the shedding of the blood of patriots and heroes. The establishment of the United States of America under the Constitution was the ultimate and greatest victory in this struggle. And now, virtually in one generation, we have trampled under our feet the blood of that covenant and considered it a thing of naught.

All one really needs to do to see the truth of the statement that all human rights are based on property rights is to ask these questions: What are the human rights which are considered more important than property rights? Do they cost money? Where will the money come from? When you have honestly answered those questions, you will know why greedy and covetous people invented the idea that "human rights are more important than property rights." You will also know that without property there can be no rights. Then it becomes a question of whether property shall be private or whether we shall continue the flight back to feudalism. You can't have it both ways; for the minute you have given the government the power to take one man's property away from him and give it to another, you have given the government all power over you to exercise at its discretion. And government bureaucrats can be as despotic as feudal lords. You can vote out politicians; but bureaucrats continue on from one administration to another. The one real restraint we can successfully place upon government is the restraint against seizing our property for the purpose of redistributing it to others considered more deserving of it. Government cannot guarantee us life. It can only guarantee to try to punish murderers and foreign aggressors. It cannot guarantee us liberty. It can only guarantee to try to defend us from those who would take our liberty away from us. But it can, with very few exceptions, guarantee us the right to own and control our property. If you will think about it, you will see that all wars are fought on and over property. Without property, life and liberty are meaningless even to the tenuous extent that they ever can exist in this mortal life.

The earth was organized from material and created in such a way that it could be inhabited. The Lord intended that his children should possess it. (1 Nephi 17:36.) Therefore, we find that everything Christians hold sacred, near, and dear to their hearts is bound to individual ownership and control of property.

Christians are taught by the Lord to defend and redeem their land, if necessary, by the shedding of blood. The Lord has given certain parcels of land to his covenant people to bring about his eternal purposes and to secure their mortal existence. When the Israelites went into the promised land, they immediately divided it up into inheritances by families. When the Nephites took over any area, they divided it up into inheritances by families. When the "Mormons" went into any part of the Great Basin, one of their first pieces of business was to follow that same old Israelite custom of dividing up the land by families. The Almighty has given divine deeds to some of his real estate. There are over 1600 references to land in the complete concordance to the Book of Mormon and the Doctrine and Covenants.

Take-off Passage

Alma 44:5.

Other Passages

1 Nephi 2:20; 13:9–20, 30; 17:23–40; 22:7; 2 Nephi 1:5–9; 3:2; 10:7–19; Enos 1:10; Mosiah 29:21; Alma 43:45–48; 3 Nephi 15:12–14; 21:4; 14:2; Doctrine and Covenants 101:8; 134:1–2. (See President David O. McKay, Conference Report, October 1962.) See also ALJ, WAR, and PI.

Study Questions

1. How do these scriptures give meaning to the long-standing teaching that the Saints should have the goal of owning their homes free of debt?
2. What security would an LDS family have in a dedicated home?
3. What are some things that are more precious than life in this state of probation?
4. When, where, and why should men risk their lives in war?
5. Why is it becoming increasingly difficult for people in America to own their homes free of debt?
6. Why does every economic problem grow instead of shrink when the government tries to solve it?
7. From what source does all wealth issue?

The Book of Mormon Can Save Us from Deception • D •

There is a difference between being deceived and making a

mistake. When you are deceived, you think you are right when you are wrong; so you are less likely to make a correction and get back on course. You go on living and doing things that are wrong, but you think they are right. Since we reap as we sow, the harvest of deception is an empty granary. Life is frustrating at best; but when we are led by men like Nehor, Sherem, Korihor, Gadianton, and Amalickiah, we are led down into destruction both temporally and spiritually. The lives of these men are case histories of deceivers and the deceived. If you will study them, you will see that many of the people of the world are being led today by men just like them.

Take-off Passage

Alma 30:53.

Other Passages

Jacob 7:18; Mosiah 7:21–23; 26:16; Alma 12:6; 3 Nephi 2:1–3; Doctrine and Covenants 10:5–29; 28:11; 45:57; 46:7–10; 50:1–27; 52:14; 54:14; 123:11–17; JS-M 1:4–10. See also KR.

Study Questions

1. Can you recall some instances in your life when you were deceived?
2. Can you name any great and good men whom historians have never identified as deceivers?
3. Which of the Ten Commandments must you break to deceive people?
4. When is it possible for a good man to do just as much damage as a willful deceiver?
5. Why is it more likely that a prophet or great patriot will be accused of deception than that a real deceiver will be so accused?

The Sure Foundation Is the Rock of Christ • ROC •

Before studying this section, the reader would do well to look up Matthew 16:16–18 in the new LDS edition of the Bible and read all the references given in the footnotes to those three verses. Many members of the Church have put forth the idea that, instead of building his Church on Peter, Jesus was saying that he would build his

Church on the "rock of revelation." It is more likely that he was saying that he would cause the Church to be built upon the rock of Christ through the individual testimonies of Jesus that the members have received through revelation. After all, we are not built upon the rock of Christ until we have the testimony of Jesus or else have that firm faith in the testimonies of those who do have the testimony of Jesus. (See Doctrine and Covenants 46:13–14; Moroni 7:32.) And without many such people in the Church it could not have triumphed over all the powers of earth and hell. The multitude of testimonies of Jesus possessed by all the valiant is the bedrock foundation upon which Christ builds his Church.

We know that he did not mean Peter as the rock upon which he would build his Church because (1) Peter was a man, and (2) Christ said, "thou art *Petros*" (masculine singular for "rock," a name often given to boys by the Greeks) "and upon this *petra*" (feminine plural for "rock," meaning "mother rock" or bedrock) "I will build my church." The passage suffers much in the common English translation. It, like many other problem passages, comes out much better in German and other languages which give nouns gender. That may be one reason why Joseph Smith, after studying German, stated a preference for the Martin Luther "translation" of the Bible.

Anyway, the doctrine about the rock of Christ is clarified in the Book of Mormon. Jesus Christ is a joy and a refuge to the Saints; but he is a "stumbling block," a "rock of offense," to those who will not be redeemed. Everyone who has become accountable must seek refuge on this rock, the sure foundation whereon the righteous build with the assurance that they cannot then fall. (They can, of course, deliberately and knowingly leap off the rock into perdition, thus committing spiritual suicide.)

Take-off Passage

Helaman 5:12.

Other Passages

2 Nephi 18:14, 15; Jacob 4:15–17; Mosiah 3:17; 4:1–7; 3 Nephi 11:39, 40; Matthew 7:13, 14; 21:42–44; Acts 4:11, 12; 1 Corinthians 3:11; Ephesians 2:20; 1 Peter 2:7, 8; Doctrine and Covenants 11:24; 18:4–5.

Study Questions

1. Why should we want to marry only those who also are founded upon the rock of Christ?

2. What relationships do you see between the principles taught in this section and those taught in the sections called MID, PD, and BA?

3. What is the difference between having moral discipline by external compulsion and by internal restraint? If a man is founded on the rock of Christ, which does he have and why?

4. Give examples of external compulsion causing moral restraint.

5. Give some examples of false, but widely accepted, theories of men or the devil from which you can be saved by being founded on the rock of Christ.

6. When was Peter founded on the rock of Christ? What difference did it make in his life? How does this illustrate that the testimony of Jesus is crucial to the survival of the Church in its purity?

The Prophets Teach Us What We Need, Not Just What We Want

• NEED •

Prophets have always offended people, and no prophet was as offensive as Jesus. We can almost say that if a prophet is not unpopular he must not be doing his job. No end of prophets have been killed in the line of duty. Being a prophet can be a deadly job if the prophet is a true prophet.

To the world and to apostates, a prophet is a good fellow as long as he is dead or minds his own business. If he is dead, those of the world can play with his words and make them say anything they want them to say. They can "pick and choose," keeping only what pleases them. But if he is living, he doesn't always "mind his own business," doesn't always oblige by restricting himself to speaking on "religious" matters. He may even correct us and tell us what he really meant when we twist his words. At election time, for example, some want prophets to keep still even though they acknowledge from time to time that elections are extremely important to the survival of the Church and to our individual lives as Saints. They do not want to believe God unless he tells them what they want to hear. We more or less permanently silenced the prophets on political issues at election time several decades ago. It is an example of the "law of Moses principle": if you refuse the greater law, you get the lesser law.

Some especially get upset if the prophets tell us what is true or false in the academic areas. We may think they are not qualified to speak—at least "not in our field." Some experts on political science want the prophets to keep still on politics. Some experts on evolution want them to keep still on evolution. Some experts on Bible interpretation want them to keep still on Bible interpretation. We hear voices which say things that mean this: "Aren't there enough things for the prophets to do without sticking their noses into our business? Let them see to their welfare programs and to the problem of sin. We will take care of the rest." So say the present-day lovers of dead or silent prophets. In the meantime, those who truly love the prophets are building up the kingdom at an accelerating rate under the direction of the prophets.

Take-off Passage

Helaman 13:24–29.

Other Passages

1 Nephi 1:4, 18–20; Jacob 7:1–23; Mosiah 12:9–17; 13:1–9; 15:11; 29:5–32; Alma 1:2–16; 30:6–60; 3 Nephi 10:11, 12; 12:1; 28:34; Exodus 4:1; 16:1–3; Isaiah 30:9–11; 2 Chronicles 36:14–21; Matthew 10:34–39; 11:7–12; 21:33–42; 22:1–10; 23:29–33; John 9:28; Acts 7:51–53.

Study Questions

1. Show from the scriptures that those who reject the prophets living today would also have rejected the prophets who are dead, whatever day they lived in.

2. Why does the Lord expect us to accept the living prophets? What does "accept" mean in this case?

3. What excuses are given for rejecting the living prophets? What does "reject" mean in this case?

4. What relationships exist between this section and the one called RVHK?

5. Why should the words of living prophets take precedence and

priority over the opinions of statesmen, philosophers, scientists, and others when the latter enter the area of revealed religion?

6. When should the scriptures affect opinions of LDS scientists on scientific matters?

7. When is the word of a prophet of God better in *any* area than that of a human expert in the same area?

8. To what dangers are we exposed when we reject the counsel of the prophets? Give historical examples, including some found in the scriptures.

The Life of a True Saint Begins with a Broken Heart and a Contrite Spirit • BHCS •

Greatness grows out of the fertile ground of meekness and humility. Even Jesus, the great creator of heaven and earth, had to descend below all things that he might rise above all things. He submitted himself to all the indignities and pain that man, the devil, the mortal milieu, and his own sorrow for the sins of the world could heap upon him. He rose triumphant to his eternal throne at the right hand of the Father, having prepared a way by which all who would might follow him there. He who would follow must go by the true way; and Jesus is the true way. (John 14:6.) One must start with an offering of a broken heart and a contrite spirit. It is the entrance fee to get into the starting gate. No repentance is a repentance, no offering is an offering, until this offering has been made.

Take-off Passage

3 Nephi 9:19–20.

Other Passages

2 Nephi 2:7; 9:42; Mosiah 4:1–2; 5:2; Helaman 8:15; 15:7–9; 3 Nephi 12:19–20; Ether 4:15; Moroni 6:2; 8:24–25; Doctrine and Covenants 20:37; 59:8; 97:8.

Study Questions

1. What is the reward of a broken heart and a contrite spirit?

2. What is the path that will lead to a broken heart and a contrite spirit?

3. Why do the scriptures call a broken heart and a contrite spirit a sacrifice? (See Alma 22:18.)

4. Why is any description of repentance incomplete unless it includes the concept of a broken heart and a contrite spirit?

5. Explain in your own words the difference between BHCS and a loss of self-respect or self-confidence, or between BHCS and having a poor self-image.

6. In what or in whom does one trust when he has experienced a broken heart?

A Good Share of the Corruption of the Bible Was by the Deletion of Plain and Precious Things

• COBD •

Joseph Smith said that we believe the Bible "as far as it is translated correctly." (Articles of Faith 1:8.) Because of this obviously rational and unimpeachable statement, devious people have accused the Mormons of not believing the Bible. Actually, we believe far more of it than any other people. Even the most fundamental of Christians are forever searching for additional light on the original text and its meaning. Some have published new "translations" in the twentieth century. Thus they demonstrate by their actions that they take exactly the same view Joseph Smith expressed in the eighth article of faith.

Judging by the nature of the work involved in Joseph Smith's inspired "translation" of the Bible, he meant that we believe the Bible to the extent that it is the same as it was originally given. Very little of the work he did could be called "translating" in the usual sense of the word. Mostly he put pack parts of the Bible that had been taken out. And he got these parts by revelation in many cases and by deductions based on revelation in others.

Nephi described the genesis of a church which was more abominable than any other church. (1 Nephi 13.) He said that after the Bible went from the Apostles to the Gentiles in purity, it was corrupted by that church. He implied that most of the damage was the deletion of plain and precious things concerning the gospel and the covenants of God.

The Book of Mormon contains a number of passages which show

that the brass plates contained information which our present Bible does not. Certain New Testament passages indicate that the Old Testament of Jesus' day and Paul's day also contained these things. For instance, Paul's allusion to the tame and wild olive trees in his letter to the Romans has frustrated the scholars because he so obviously expected those who read his message to know what he was talking about. Perhaps they had Zenos' account. (See Jacob 5.) Besides Zenos, the Book of Mormon tells us about the writings of Ezias, Zenock, and Neum, whose books were in the brass plates.

We have to be careful that we do not overplay the idea that the Bible has been corrupted by deletions and changes. It is very probable that the Lord outsmarted the adversary and arranged to have the Bible preserved in that manner and to that degree that would best serve his purposes. We can safely believe almost every verse that is left. Only a few passages are wrong enough to create any problems.

President J. Reuben Clark, Jr., made some wise suggestions about the Bible, the essence of which follows: (1) Stay with the King James version, because the men who made that translation were believers who would only rarely deliberately translate figuratively instead of literally. (2) Accept almost everything you understand in the Bible unless modern revelation or unimpeachable scholarship has shown it to be false. (3) Question or withhold judgment on those ideas which appear only in a single Bible passage and have no confirmation in modern revelation.

Take-off Passage

3 Nephi 10:14–17.

Other Passages

1 Nephi 13:20–32; 19:10–21; 2 Nephi 3:5–22; Jacob 5; 6:1; Alma 33:3, 13, 15; 34:7; 46:23–27; Helaman 8:19, 20; 15:11; Luke 24:25–27, 44–47; Romans 11:16–25; 1 Corinthians 15:3, 4; Galatians 3:8; Moses; Abraham; Joseph Smith—Matthew 1; Doctrine and Covenants 45:15–60.

Study Questions

1. List six important concepts concerning the mission of Joseph who was sold into Egypt which cannot be found in the present Bible. In what two places can Latter-day Saints find them?

2. How do the ideas and scriptures given in this section help you to understand the Bible better? Give examples.

3. Does it appear to you that Joseph Smith could have had the training, background, and time to formulate the teachings and ideas pointed out in this section without divine help?

4. Why were the plain and precious things taken out of the Bible?

5. What evidence do we have that the Old Testament has been changed? the New Testament?

The Sermon on the Mount Is Indicative of the Path a Converted Saint Should Follow • PATH •

Jesus "went up into" the mountain, not up on it. He went up there to get away from the multitude, not to address them. He gave the sermon only to the Twelve to begin with, because they were the only disciples he had at that time. And the sermon was meant only for the ears of the believers. For one thing, the outsiders would find it too insulting if they understood it. For another, it contains instructions meant only for certain General Authorities—those things about "taking no thought for the morrow," for example. And, again, it is meaningless to anyone but a Saint who has "entered the gate," has experienced a broken heart and a contrite spirit, and has been spiritually reborn.

This section leads to an understanding of how the "redeemed man," "man of the Spirit," "new man," and so on, should live. An interesting fact is revealed in the vision of the tree, the river, the path, and the rod of iron: No matter how good his intentions, a man cannot remain on the good path without having hold of the rod of iron—which is the word of God. This is why those who are puffed up with their learning or their riches cannot be saved unless they "cast these things away, and consider themselves fools before God." (2 Nephi 9:42.)

Take-off Passage

3 Nephi 12, 13, 14.

Other Passages

1 Nephi 8:2–35; 2 Nephi 31:5–18; 33:9; Mosiah 4:4–30; Alma 5:26–43; 13:27–30; 34:28–30; 38:10–14; 41:14, 15; 3 Nephi 12, 13, 14 (except 13:25–34, which in our day probably applies to certain General Authorities only); Moroni 7.

Study Questions

1. Do you believe, after studying these scriptures, that it is possible for unredeemed mankind to live the morals of the Sermon on the Mount?

2. List as many reasons as you can to show that many who think of themselves as Christians trying to live the Sermon on the Mount have not yet entered the gate. Relate this idea to the section called JG concerning the purpose of the Book of Mormon. Relate it to MID.

3. What principles of the gospel should the young people of the Church learn and accept if they are to acquire the motivation and self-control necessary to follow the path the Lord has outlined for the Saints?

4. Which corrections or clarifications of the Sermon on the Mount given in the Nephite version have a serious bearing on Christian conduct and ethics? Which have a bearing on the conduct and ethics of members of the Church who are not General Authorities?

Some Corruption of the Bible Has Been Caused by Changes in the Text • COBC •

The main trouble with our present-day Bible is that many plain and precious things have been taken out. (See ABT and COBD.) In general, what is left is highly reliable, but there are some changes which have corrupted the Bible. For instance, more than half of the several hundred verses of Isaiah quoted in the Book of Mormon are somewhat different from the same verses in the King James version. Most of the differences are not significant, but some are. One such example is included in the "other passages" below. Also, the Book of Mormon sheds significant light on changes that may have been made in the Bible version of the Sermon on the Mount. (3 Nephi 12, 13, 14.)

Take-off Passage

3 Nephi 12:3 (Matthew 5:3).

Other Passages

1 Nephi 20:1 (Isaiah 48:1); 3 Nephi 12:17–19 (Matthew 5:17–19); 3 Nephi 12:22 (Matthew 5:22); 3 Nephi 12:29, 30 (Matthew 5:29, 30); 3 Nephi 13:25 (Matthew 6:25); 3 Nephi 14:1 (Matthew 7:1); Moses (Genesis 1–6:13). (A good source for further study of this subject is Sidney B. Sperry, *Our Book of Mormon* [Salt Lake City: Bookcraft, 1947].)

Study Questions

1. How does this section demonstrate to you the principle outlined in 1 Nephi 13:37–40 regarding the relationships between the Bible and the Book of Mormon? Consider this question also with reference to 2 Nephi 3:12 and Mormon 7:8–9.
2. How do these changes supplement your conviction that Joseph Smith translated an ancient record by divine power?
3. How might the Bible version of the Sermon on the Mount in its present form seriously mislead some in their practice of Christianity? How might it be used incorrectly to support an anti-free enterprise mentality?

The Book of Mormon Proves That Christ Is the God of the Old Testament

• CGOT •

When Jesus visited the Nephites, he informed them that he was the personage who gave the law to Moses. Elsewhere the Book of Mormon identifies him as the Creator. Abinadi, in fact, gave these four reasons why Jesus has the title of Father: (1) as the heir of his Father or inheritor of the title, (2) as the complete and constant agent of his Father, acting in his behalf, (3) as the Creator or "Father" of heaven and earth, and (4) as the Father of the faithful, those who are begotten sons and daughters of God through spiritual rebirth.

There are many names for Deity. Probably most of them could be used for either the Father or the Son. In the LDS Church we frequently refer to our Heavenly Father by the name of *Elohim* when we want to be sure there is no mistake about the identity of the person about whom we are talking. In the same manner and for the same reasons, we commonly call Jesus *Jehovah.* The use of the word *Elohim* in this manner is arbitrary, and the name *Jehovah* could just as well be applied to the Father as to the Son. However, it is true that the personage who identified himself as Jehovah was usually, if not always, Jesus. But since he was always acting on behalf of the Father, he could have been using a name that applied as well to the Father as to the Son. *Jehovah* is probably the first person, singular, present form of the verb *to be* in the Hebrew language. Most likely it simply means "I AM."

To most churches in the Christian world—and especially to the Jehovah Witnesses—Jehovah is the "God of the Old Testament" and is identified with the Father. Of course, it is a moot point in the case of all but the Jehovah Witnesses; because most Christians do not distinguish between the Father and the Son in the way we do. They think of them as different "masks" or manifestations of the same universal spirit that has no substance or form unless it assumes a form for a special purpose. But the main point of doctrine in the Jehovah Witness church is that Jehovah is the Father, the eternal God. They believe Jesus is a later and lesser God, and that both are immaterial, all-pervading "spirits" in their present state, with separate identities. Thus the Jehovah Witnesses also take emphatic issue with the LDS position even though in a slightly different way than do the Catholics and Protestants.

To a Latter-day Saint who understands the content and purpose of the Book of Mormon, the answer is simple. There is no need for argument. Just find out that the Book of Mormon is true and then read what Jesus said in Third Nephi.

Take-off Passage

3 Nephi 15:5.

Other Passages

1 Nephi 6:4; 17:25–30; Jacob 4:4, 12; Alma 39:17; 19:7–13; Mosiah 3:5; 13:13; 15:1–6; Helaman 8:14–23; Ether 3:15, 16; Isaiah 6:1–6; John 4:25, 26; 8:58; 12:41.

Study Questions

1. Why is this concept important in discussing the gospel with a member of the Jewish faith?

2. From the CGOT vantage point, when did Christianity begin and what does this mean to the conventional theory of all religions evolving from the simple to the complex, from lower forms to higher forms?

3. What does the Book of Mormon say about Christ's omnipotence and omniscience? How does knowing that he is the God of the Old Testament help prove his omniscience and omnipotence?

4. How does this section help prove the fallacy of the idea that the God of the Old Testament was a cruel God and that Jesus introduced a more loving God?

5. Make up a step-by-step argument or list of agreements by which you would show someone that Jesus is the Jehovah who gave the law of Moses.

The Book of Mormon Reveals That America Is That Land of Joseph That Was Given to Him in Addition to His Old World Inheritance • ALJ •

A recurring theme in the Book of Mormon is that America is the land of Joseph. Lehi and Ishmael were both descendants of Joseph, the son of Israel (Jacob). Through them and their seed, Joseph inherited this land. But the blessing does not stop there. We are told in the Book of Mormon that the posterity of Lehi and Ishmael would regain the covenant right to the land of America in the last days through the instrumentality of the "Gentiles," and that the "believing Gentiles" would be numbered among the seed of Joseph and also inherit this land. First the Gentiles were to be led to America by the Spirit, where they would drive back and dispossess the Lamanites. Then the gospel was to be restored to these "Gentiles" and go from them to the seed of Lehi. Apparently the Nephites were not told that these "believing Gentiles" would also be, for the most part, literal descendants of Joseph. The Lord explained this legal heirship of the "believing Gentiles" in these words:

> Therefore, thus saith the Lord unto you, with whom the priesthood hath continued through the lineage of your fathers—
>
> For ye are lawful heirs, according to the flesh, and have been hid from the world with Christ in God—

> Therefore your life and the priesthood have remained, and must needs remain through you and your lineage until the restoration of all things spoken by the mouths of all the holy prophets since the world began.
>
> Therefore, blessed are ye if ye continue in my goodness, a light unto the Gentiles, and through this priesthood, a savior unto my people Israel. (Doctrine and Covenants 86:8–11.)

Remember that the birthright was Joseph's through his sons, Ephraim and Manasseh. The birthright is the keys of the Melchizedek Priesthood. It is not the land inheritance. All thirteen tribes (counting two for Joseph) received land inheritances in one way or another. Levi's inheritance was scattered in parcels throughout all Israel; but also that tribe, as the priest tribe, was supported by the other tribes to a great extent. But the keys of the priesthood was Joseph's birthright. Thus, Ephraim and Manasseh must be gathered first so that they can "push the tribes together to the ends of the earth," one end being Jerusalem, the other end being Zion.

Jacob, in blessing his twelve sons, promised himself an additional blessing above Abraham's and Isaac's through Joseph, the one "separated from his brethren." In connection with this blessing, he called Joseph "a fruitful bough by a well, whose branches run over the wall." And he spoke of the land "of the everlasting hills," a clear reference to America or to a land far away at the ends of the earth. Joseph's additional land inheritance was partially fulfilled when Ephraim and Manasseh obtained separate inheritances in the Old World. But, just as Joseph was separated from the rest in Egypt, so he was to be separated from his brethren at the other end of the earth.

Take-off Passage

3 Nephi 15:12–15.

Other Passages

1 Nephi 2:20; 13:9–23, 30, 33; 14:1–7; 17:23–41; 18:23; 22:7; 2 Nephi 3:2, 5; 4:1–2; 10:10–20; Enos 10; Alma 46:23–25; 3 Nephi 20:27; Ether 1:38; 2:7–12; 13:6–8; Doctrine and Covenants 101:80; Genesis 49:22–26; Deuteronomy 33:15–16; *History of the Church,* 6:318–19; Mark E. Petersen, *Joseph of Egypt,* chapters 32–34; *JD,* 1:248–58.

Study Questions

1. What were the Lord's purposes in giving America to the tribe of Joseph for an inheritance?
2. What were and are the conditions of Joseph's inheriting the land of America?
3. What happens to a "Gentile" to make him a rightful heir to Joseph's blessings?
4. What would be the difference in America surrendering its sovereignty to a one-world government designed by men and in surrendering its sovereignty to the kingdom and government of God during the Millennium?
5. How can this section help you better understand your political responsibilities?
6. What did the establishment of the United States of America have to do with the restoration of the gospel?

The Day of the Lamanite Is Dawning • DL •

Early in President Spencer W. Kimball's administration, he announced that there were then 500,000 "Lamanites" in the Church. Most of them were "south of the border," of course. And few were what have been called full-blooded "Indians." In fact, such people are becoming more and more rare relative to the population of the Americas as a whole.

There have been "Indians" in the Church since Joseph Smith's day, but not many. As late as the 1930s the number was negligible. Then, in little more than a generation, the number who could claim descendancy from Lehi and Ishmael rose to over a half a million. And it is still rising.

In some ways, it is unfortunate that we call them "Lamanites." When peace and righteousness broke down in America in about A.D. 300, those who rebelled against the Church and the prophets called themselves Lamanites as an act of rebellion. But they probably were as much of a mixture of ancestry as were those who called themselves Nephites. In other words, when these two appellations were revived, they had more of a political and religious significance than a genealogical significance. This is borne out in how the Lord speaks of them in section 3 of the Doctrine and Covenants:

> Nevertheless, my work shall go forth, for inasmuch as the knowledge of a Savior has come unto the world, through the testimony of the Jews, even so shall the knowledge of a Savior come unto my people—
>
> And to the Nephites, and the Jacobites, and the Josephites, and the Zoramites, through the testimony of their fathers—
>
> And this testimony shall come to the knowledge of the Lamanites, and the Lemuelites, and the Ishmaelites, who dwindled in unbelief because of the iniquity of their fathers, whom the Lord has suffered to destroy their brethren the Nephites, because of their iniquities and their abominations.
>
> And for this very purpose are these plates preserved, which contain these records—that the promises of the Lord might be fulfilled which he made to his people;
>
> And that the Lamanites might come to the knowledge of their fathers, and that they might know the promises of the Lord, and that they may believe the gospel and rely upon the merits of Jesus Christ, and be glorified through faith in his name, and that through their repentance they might be saved. Amen. (Verses 16–20.)

The above passage at least implies that converted descendants of Lehi and Ishmael might as well call themselves Nephites as Lamanites. Most of all, they should call themselves Christians. And they were promised that, when that happened to them, their day would have arrived. The number of Lehi's descendants in the Church must be now (1986) close to a million. Their history was all foretold in the patriarchal blessings of Lehi to his and Ishmael's children. The best of those promises are now being fulfilled. The "day of the Lamanite" is dawning with great promise and glory.

Take-off Passage

3 Nephi 16:11–12.

Other Passages

Book of Mormon Title Page; 1 Nephi 15:13–17; 22:8; 2 Nephi 4 and 5; 30:3–5; Jacob 3:6; Alma 9:16–17; 3 Nephi 21:20–29; Mormon 5:19–20; Doctrine and Covenants 3:16–20.

Study Questions

1. What is the significance of the intermarriage practices of Latin Americans? How was this implied in the tame and wild olive trees allegory in the book of Jacob? See if you can find some pertinent verses.

2. What have you learned from this section that you did not know already about the "blossoming" of the people we commonly call Lamanites?

3. Trace the different meanings of the title "Lamanite" in the Book of Mormon.

4. What avenues are open to you to help the "Lamanites" reach their full potential?

5. What evidences do you know of which show that the "Lamanites," as a total people, did not apostatize any further from original Christianity than did the Gentiles? How do language barriers affect our perceptions about the remnants of Christianity among the "Indians"?

6. What are some changes you have seen among the "Lamanites" during your lifetime?

7. Find statements from at least three Presidents of the Church which bear on "Lamanite" destiny.

The Bread and Water of the Sacrament Have Separate Significances As Well As Common Significances

• B & W •

Some have supposed that the atonement of Christ was performed simply to break the bands of death and bring about the universal resurrection. These are the people who are most likely to emphasize that we "save ourselves." They give Paul's statement about "working out our salvation with fear and trembling" a different meaning than the one he intended. They overlook the fact that good works are the result of the rebirth. Good works are a part of the natural life of the "new man." These good works do not pay for bad works. The sins we have committed can be paid for only by Christ. Our good works do not "earn" or "merit" anything, even if we must do them in order to become fit subjects of the heavenly King. The scriptures are quite clear in showing that not all are saved and that those who are saved are saved through Christ, or, in other words, cleansed through his blood. Since all are resurrected, it follows that Christ did more than bring about a resurrection. And his time in

Gethsemane was not just an hour of decision, as many in other Christian churches believe.

The two purposes (resurrection and atonement) of Jesus' mission are pointed out to us in the two elements and two prayers of what we call "the sacrament." Also, the prophets have clearly taught that Jesus brought about both an atonement and a resurrection, as the following verses indicate:

> Wherefore, beloved brethren, be reconciled unto him through the atonement of Christ, his Only Begotten Son, and ye may obtain a resurrection, according to the power of the resurrection which is in Christ, and be presented as the first-fruits of Christ unto God, having faith, and obtained a good hope of glory in him before he manifesteth himself in the flesh.
>
> And now, beloved, marvel not that I tell you these things; for why not speak of the atonement of Christ, and attain to a perfect knowledge of him, as to attain to the knowledge of a resurrection and the world to come? (Jacob 4:11–12.)

While the Atonement made the resurrection possible, it still has a greater function than just resurrection. And that is the reason for both bread and wine or water. The bread represents the body or the resurrection; the water represents the blood or the Atonement.

Take-off Passage

3 Nephi 18:1–11.

Other Passages

2 Nephi 2:10; 10:25; 25:23; Jacob 4:11, 12; Mosiah 3:15–18; 4:2, 6, 7; Alma 5:27; 21:9; 24:13; 33:22; 3 Nephi 20:8; Moroni 4, 5, 7:41; John 6:53. (See James E. Talmage, *Jesus the Christ* [Salt Lake City: Deseret Book Co., 1962], ch. 33: "The Last Supper and the Betrayal.")

Study Questions

1. Why do we have two emblems in the sacrament? Why not just partake of one, perhaps the bread, and do it in remembrance of the atonement of Christ?
2. With what crucial events do you associate the bread?
3. With what crucial events do you associate the water? How are these events related to each other?

4. How do the events in questions 2 and 3 relate to the plan of salvation and Christ as our Redeemer?

5. Why do many in the world think Gethsemane was merely an hour of decision? How do you know they are wrong?

6. Find two passages of scripture in which Christ implied that his greatest suffering was in Gethsemane.

7. How can you demonstrate that the words *salvation* and *redemption* ordinarily do not refer to resurrection per se when used in the scriptures?

The True Saints and the True Church Must Be Called After the Name of Christ

• NAME •

There is a name that all the faithful must bear and not be ashamed of, and that name is the name of Christ. That is the name King Benjamin promised the faithful. That is the name Abinadi reminded them of. That is the name Christ himself designated as the only name for his Church. "There is none other name under heaven given among men, whereby we must be saved." (Acts 4:12.)

Take-off Passage

3 Nephi 27:3–9.

Other Passages

Mosiah 1:11, 12; 18:17; 25:19–24; 26:17–28; Alma 46:12–18; Helaman 5:7–15; 3 Nephi 20:39; Matthew 10:32, 33; Mark 8:38; Luke 9:26; Acts 11:26.

Study Questions

1. What must one do to rightfully and totally claim the name of Christ?

2. What difference is there between being a Christian, as the world defines it, and taking upon oneself the name of Christ as outlined in the Book of Mormon?

3. What fruits from the churches of Christendom make it impossible for them to be the true church of Christ?

4. What are some of the differences between our definition of what constitutes a Christian and what the world calls a Christian? What does the bodily state of Christ and his Father have to do with this?

5. What is the significance of the fact that no church in Joseph Smith's day had a legal claim on the use of the title, the Church of Jesus Christ?

6. Why is neither the Church nor its members ever perfect? Why should we carefully explain what we mean—or never say it—when we say, "I know this is the only true church?" What do some others think we mean that we do not mean?

The Doctrine or Gospel of Christ Embraces the First Principles or the Good News of How to Be Saved Through Christ • DGC •

We live in a happy and blessed time, for the fulness of the new and everlasting covenant is available to all mankind. That hasn't always been the case. In fact, under the law of Moses, not even the fulness of the gospel covenant was available. During such times, those deprived of a fulness have to look forward to a time when their posterity will provide the rest through temple work.

Even now, when we have a fulness, we enter into this fulness in three steps: first we enter into the gospel covenant, then the priesthood covenant (fully entered into by both men and women through the endowment), and finally the fulness is offered through the marriage covenant.

Every covenant binds both parties to certain obligations and rewards. It also provides a punishment for failure on the part of either party. Of course, God never fails.

The purpose of the gospel covenant is to obtain a remission of sins. The other covenants provide even higher rewards; but they are based upon the gospel covenant. Without a remission of sins, there can be no other rewards. Also, when we have taken upon ourselves the higher obligations we come into greater and more numerous opportunities to sin and fail. Progress always includes risk.

The principles and ordinances that have the greatest bearing on —those that are included in—the gospel covenant are: (1) the fall of man and the predicament of fallen man (included by inference only, as it is really the "bad news" that necessitates the "good news"); (2) the doctrine of eternal judgments (also technically a part of the bad news); (3) the Atonement; (4) the Resurrection; (5) faith in the Lord Jesus Christ (which is really faith in his atonement and resurrection); (6) repentance, including the broken heart and the contrite spirit; (7) baptism by immersion by proper authority for the remission of sins; (8) the laying on of hands for the gift of the Holy Ghost; and (9) the necessity and meaning of enduring with faith in Christ and with repentance to the end of this mortal life.

What it boils down to is that the gospel is the "good news" about the plan of complete escape from the predicament and judgments of fallen man.

Take-off Passage

3 Nephi 27:13–21.

Other Passages

2 Nephi 31:5–18; 33:9; Jacob 7:6; 3 Nephi 11:31–41; Matthew 7:13, 14; Hebrews 5:11–14; 6:1–6; Joseph Smith 2:34; Doctrine and Covenants 10:46–70; 18:4; 20:8, 9; 27:5; 39:5, 6; 42:12; 76:40–42; 88:17–22.

Study Questions

1. What relationships exist among the following: the gospel of Christ, milk before the meat, and missionary work? (See Alma 22:12–18; 1 Corinthians 2:1–6; 3:1–5; 15:1–6.)
2. How does the meaning of the word *gospel,* as herein defined, differ from the popular meaning as we commonly use it in the Church? How does this scriptural meaning clear up some mistaken ideas created by the popular meaning?
3. Where does the Doctrine and Covenants tell us to go to find a fulness of the gospel as herein defined?
4. What is the Book of Mormon concept of the source of the gospel as compared to the concept of the source of the gospel that would equate *gospel* with truth in general?
5. Demonstrate that the passages given in this section equate gospel of Christ, doctrine of Christ, and law of Christ. (Remember that, if a = b and a = c, then b = c.)

A Saint Is One Who Has Been Sanctified by the Blood of Christ • SB •

The word *saint* comes from the same root as *sanctify* and *sanctification.* Thus a Saint is one who has been sanctified by Christ. In antiquity, as now, all members of the Church of Jesus Christ were addressed as Saints. That is because it was—and is—assumed that, when they were baptized, they had believed and repented fully and were therefore sanctified.

The scriptures speak of two types of sanctification. One is sanctification by the Spirit. When we are born again and receive the new Spirit (the gift of the Holy Ghost), we are regenerated or made over into new creatures—at least, this process begins. This is possible only because of the atonement of Christ. In a sense the Spirit sanctifies us because the old wicked spirit of the carnal man is "rooted out of [our] breast." (Alma 22:15.) Now we are less disposed to do evil, but there is still the problem of satisfying the demands of the law for the sins we have committed. As soon as a sin is committed, it becomes a part of the past which must be accounted for. In the present, we may be better. We may never commit that sin again. But no amount of good deeds satisfy the law for the evil deeds that have been committed. This is where sanctification by blood, the blood of Christ, comes in. It pays for the past in the case of the truly penitent. Sanctification by the Spirit and by the blood work hand in hand to purify and redeem our souls.

Take-off Passage

3 Nephi 27:19.

Other Passages

1 Nephi 12:10, 11; Mosiah 3:11–15; Alma 5:21, 27; 13:11; 21:9; 34:8–13, 36; Moroni 10:33; Moses 6:60.

Study Questions

1. What relationship do you see between the principles herein taught and those found under B&W and RJM?
2. Why is Christ the only one who can and will sanctify a qualified candidate of the human race?

3. How does our obedience to law relate to the merits of Christ in the process of salvation?

4. Why would sanctification by the Spirit be inadequate, if not impossible, if there were no sanctification by blood?

A Saint Is One Who Has Been Sanctified by the Spirit • SS •

Sanctification by the Spirit commences at rebirth and should go on until the death of the mortal body. Indeed, for all we know, it may be a continuing part of eternal life for the faithful. We can stop the process, of course, by our sin or rebellion. The extent to which we are sanctified by the Spirit is very much up to us. (See also the note on sanctification by blood in the preceding section.)

Take-off Passage

3 Nephi 27:20.

Other Passages

2 Nephi 31:17; Alma 5:54; 13:12; Helaman 3:35; 3 Nephi 28:39; Moroni 8:26; 10:32; Moses 1:10–15, 31; 6:61; Doctrine and Covenants 20:30–34.

Study Questions

1. What does the principle of sanctification by the Spirit have to do with correct living?

2. How does being sanctified by the Spirit prepare one to live in God's presence?

3. Describe the relationship between sanctification by the Spirit and sanctification by the blood of Christ.

4. Does the Spirit pay for our sins in the process of sanctification by the Spirit?

5. Why is it not possible to have one form of sanctification without the other?

Without Continual Revelation There Is No True Christian Life • CR •

The Book of Mormon teaches that any person who does not enjoy continual revelation or who rejects the revelations of God as given through the living prophets and the accepted scriptures is in great trouble here on earth and in the hereafter. The Book of Mormon, its contents, and its coming forth demonstrate what the word *revelation* means and how revelation operates. (Doctrine and Covenants 20:6–30.)

It takes individual revelation to be saved. It takes revelation to understand revelation. It takes revelation to know a revelation. It takes revelation to have priesthood authority. It takes revelation to live the way Christ wants us to live. It takes revelation to do missionary work. It takes revelation to be converted. It takes revelation to run the day-to-day affairs of the kingdom of God on earth.

Every way and every time the Holy Ghost touches our lives it is revelation by definition, because it is some form or other of communication from God. The Holy Ghost himself is a member of the Godhead and he speaks only the words the Father and Son give him to speak. If we are to be saved, the Holy Ghost must touch our lives continually. Indeed, all of this revelation must be continual.

Take-off Passage

3 Nephi 29.

Other Passages

1 Nephi 10:22; 2 Nephi 27:7, 21–27; Alma 4:20; 5:44–48; 6:8; 17:1–3; 23:6; Helaman 4:11, 12; 3 Nephi 5:13–18; 26:12; Mormon 8:22–38; Doctrine and Covenants 1:29; 6:22–24; 8:1–3; 11:25; 17:6–9; 18:1–5. (See RVHK, NEED.)

Study Questions

1. Identify at least five instances when missionaries in the Book of Mormon were helped in their labors by immediate personal revelation.

2. Identify at least three cases in the Book of Mormon when converts felt the power of revelation.

3. If a person presented Revelation 22:18–20 to you as proof that revelation has ceased, how would you use the Book of Mormon to show him the error of his position?

4. If you were teaching a person who was indifferent or lukewarm to your message, how would you use the Book of Mormon to interest him in his need for Christ?

5. How does the Book of Mormon prove "that God does inspire men and call them to his holy work"? (Doctrine and Covenants 20:11.)

The Book of Mormon Came by Divine Power to Confound the Wise and Learned • BDP •

What people believe about the nature of man, the universe, and the Supreme Being affects their conduct. And what people believe about these things is determined by the authorities they listen to and have faith in. In a supposedly enlightened age, such as we call ours, if one man can defend his ideas about man, the universe, and God better than someone else can, he tends to feel more vindicated in his belief. Of course, in the end true faith is justified; but the modern mind, being what it is, insists on fortifying its faith with reason.

One of the compelling qualities of the Book of Mormon is that it leaves you with no middle ground. Either it is a divine revelation or it is a fraud. If one finds it to be a divine revelation, he has to accept it as the final word on any subject upon which it comments. It confounds false doctrine, lays down contentions, and establishes peace. (2 Nephi 3:12.) This fact is abundantly attested to in its pages, wherein it is made clear that the book is a divine book, revealed by divine power. That is, God has made sure of its reliability. (See also this book's Introduction, much of which is on this same subject.)

Take-off Passage

Mormon 8:12–26.

Other Passages

Preface to the Book of Mormon; 1 Nephi 9; 13:39, 40; 2 Nephi

3:7, 11, 12, 18–21; Words of Mormon 1:4–8; Mormon 3:17–21; 8:34, 35; 9:32–37; Moroni 7:35; Doctrine and Covenants 1:29, 30; 3:16–20; 5:3–12; 6:15–17, 22, 23; 8:1–3; 17:6; 18:1–3; 20:6–34.

Study Questions

1. What is to be gained by studying the Book of Mormon if one is eclectic in his attitude toward what it teaches? How does such picking and choosing of only what is intellectually or socially pleasing on a personal basis merely confirm the confusion that already exists in the world?
2. Why is it impossible for an eclectic to find the truth that he needs in order to be saved? In other words, where there is no final judge of truth and error, why can we not expect personal opinion and confusion to be overcome?
3. How can the Book of Mormon as a divine revelation settle conflicting opinions and doctrines on fundamental issues that exist in the world today?
4. How does rejection of the doctrine of a universal flood demonstrate rejection of the Book of Mormon? How does rejection of the Genesis account of the origin and fall of man demonstrate rejection of the Book of Mormon? How does rejection of the Book of Mormon affect the value of membership in the Church?
5. Construct an argument to show that the Book of Mormon requires acceptance of the United States Constitution given by the Founding Fathers.
6. How can the ideas in this section be useful in missionary work?

The Book of Mormon Was Written for Our Time • FOT •

We must look at the significance of the Book of Mormon from many angles. In the previous section (BDP), we presented it as the foundation of authority for the restoration of the gospel and for the establishment of the Church of Jesus Christ in these last days. In this section, our emphasis is on the currency of its message. In the next section, we will emphasize the fact that each person must take its message personally. These ideas, together with other approaches to, or aspects of, the Book of Mormon, were dealt with in much greater detail in the introduction to this book. The reader will understand these three sections (BDP, FOT, and WTI) better if he reviews the introduction.

The Book of Mormon was deliberately and specifically written for our time. Its pages are mostly devoid of history, geography, technology, and so on, by commandment. That is, the Lord told the writers to leave these things out, for the most part. It would have been impossible, of course, to leave out every detail about such things. But as far as possible the writers, under divine guidance, wrote a universal message. What they wrote is as useful to one segment of the "family of all the earth" as another. More than that, the book is liberally sprinkled with statements directed specifically at modern Lamanites, modern Gentiles, modern Jews, and all the modern people of the earth. These statements are of the order: "God hath shown you to me." "I know your doings." "I will meet you before the judgment bar of God and you will be judged by the things I have written." And so on. They carry the idea that the Lord is not only speaking to us but he is also telling us exactly what we need to hear. To think of the Book of Mormon as anything but a message to our day is like mistakenly driving into a cul-de-sac. You are only going to have to turn around and find the right way.

One of the greatest fallacies of our time is the mistaken and dangerous notion that progress demands that old religious ideals be set aside simply because they are old. The Ten Commandments are thought to be no longer current. We have "progressed" beyond such old mores. The pundits of the arts, of the media, of the academic community, and of the political scene attempt to promote, under the guise of progress, such old and wicked practices as homosexual rights and abortion. They destroy the family in the name of progress. They deny the reality and validity of God's laws in the relationships of the sexes. They attempt to destroy or regulate social and economic laws. Somehow they seem to think that the passage of time is synonymous with the march of progress. The truth is that all men are fallen through Adam. No man can be saved except through Christ. The Ten Commandments and the Sermon on the Mount are as current at the end of time as at the beginning of time. That is what the Book of Mormon brings firmly home to the person who finds out that it is true and came the way Joseph Smith said it did. Such a person can read the Book of Mormon and see that *U.S. News and World Report* is no more current than Alma and Helaman. "There is nothing new under the sun." "That which hath been is now; and that which is to be hath already been." Alma and Helaman are talking about the same kind of events and problems as are constantly before us in the modern news. However, the Book of Mormon has the answers and the warnings applicable to our day so that we can avoid making the same mistakes if we will but apply the book to our time.

Take-off Passage

Mormon 8:34–35.

Other Passages

Title Page of the Book of Mormon; 1 Nephi 13:30–42; 19:23; 22:8–11; 2 Nephi 3:11–12 (whole chapter is applicable); 26:14; 29; 3 Nephi 21:1–9; Ether 12:38–41; Moroni 10:27–29.

Study Questions

1. What messages have you found in the Book of Mormon that are applicable to your current personal problems?
2. What messages have you found in the Book of Mormon that are applicable to current national problems? to international problems?
3. Have any of these messages changed your life?
4. What messages have you found for the future in the Book of Mormon?
5. What is the greatest proof you have found that the Book of Mormon was written for our day?

The Book of Mormon Was Written to the Individual • WTI •

Many people make the mistake of thinking there are such things as a collective mentality, collective guilt, and collective responsibility. But all minds are single. All guilt belongs to individuals. No one is responsible for anyone else's sins. Many may unite in committing an atrocity; but each person involved is responsible for his own decision to be involved. The Lord may address a multitude; but he always is talking to each individual separately. When a nation decides to appropriate money through taxes, individuals earn and pay the money. There is no formless mass or anonymous entity that vicariously suffers all this pain and deprivation. Every dime spent by the government was taken from some individual. And since all taxes are regressive, it is the poor who pay the highest percentage of tax on income. Insofar as they receive unearned benefits from "government" funds, many of them got into this tax predicament through greed, envy, wilful ignorance, and other sins or shortcomings—all of which are individual. Some, of course, are not greedy, envious, or ignorant. They suffer through the greed, envy, and ignorance of their fellow beings. But these suffer only in this life if they individually follow the instructions of the Lord given in the Book of Mormon.

In many recent Church manuals there has been a section called "Likening the Scriptures unto Us." (This idea comes from 1 Nephi 19:23.) We can, of course, liken the family of Lehi unto our families. We can liken the Nephite church unto our church. We can liken the kingmen and Gadiantons unto the fascists and socialists in our society. We can liken the Anti-Christs unto the Mormon apostates and critics. And so on. But if we look deeper than the surface, we have to see individual sin and individual goodness. Of course, the idea is to look at ourselves—each individual should look at himself or herself. That is where knowledge begins. That is where sin begins. That is where repentance begins. We can join study groups; but we can learn only as individuals. We can join motivational groups; but we improve only as individuals. "Seeking with real intent" is done only on an individual basis, even if several sincerely do it at the same time. If you are to reform the world, you start with yourself, then work on your spouse, children, ward, stake, and so on. But you follow the rules all the way. (See also BDP, FOT, and Introduction to this book.)

Take-off Passage

Mormon 8:34, 35.

Other Passages

Preface to the Book of Mormon; 1 Nephi 13:39–42; 2 Nephi 3, 27; 3 Nephi 5:8–18; Mormon 7:8–10; 8:12–35; 9:34–37; Doctrine and Covenants 1:29; 3:16–20; 5; 6:14–24.

Study Questions

1. What would you tell a friend or a child is the most efficient and productive way to study the Book of Mormon?
2. Give some examples from the Book of Mormon of individuals who first reconciled themselves to Christ and then helped others.

3. Relate Oliver Cowdery's conversion to Moroni 10:4–5. (See D&C 6.)

4. Do you feel that you have spent enough time studying the Book of Mormon to allow it to accomplish its mission in you?

5. List the objectives you think the Lord had in mind for you when he caused the Book of Mormon to be written and translated.

6. How does the reaching of these objectives by individuals help groups? What groups?

The Gadianton "Combination" Was a Political Conspiracy Against Freedom and Christ • GC •

One of the definitions for *conspiracy* in *Webster's Third New International Dictionary* is "a striking concurrence of tendencies, circumstances, or phenomena as though in planned accord." The Book of Mormon states that there will be secret combinations among the Gentiles in the last days that will seek "to overthrow the freedom of all lands, nations, and countries." (Ether 8:25.) This work of the devil was clearly to be a threat to America. The Book of Mormon and the Doctrine and Covenants teach that the founding and success of the United States, as provided by the Constitution and envisioned by the Founding Fathers, are inseparably connected with Christianity and the mission of the Lord's true church in the latter days. (3 Nephi 21:4.) As President Ezra Taft Benson has often said, "America is the Lord's base of latter-day operations."

A lot of Church members make the mistake of thinking that the Gadianton conspiracy (conspiracy is what "combination" meant to the Nephites) is confined to the actions of the so-called Mafia, or underworld, but such is not the case. It may very well always be so in the beginning. It certainly is true that the underworld always gets involved in wicked politics. But the Book of Mormon shows us that it was a political conspiracy which took over the nation and ruled it. And the people supported these systems. One clue is in the expression "the use of power to get gain." Gadianton's band started as outlaws—murderers and robbers. But their goal always was legitimacy. In effect, they said, "Vote for me and I will confiscate the wealth of our enemies and give it to you." That made robbery legal. When a government has the power to redistribute the wealth, freedom is gone. Morality is gone. And Gadianton is there. We see all this when we understand the Book of Mormon.

We must not think of ourselves as poor, duped victims of a very few wicked leaders. One of the greatest Protestant historians and theologians of our time, Rousas John Rushdoony, has correctly pointed out that no wicked conspiracy has ever succeeded without a very large backing. In fact, he suggests that this backing has to be a majority. Let us not forget that the prophets have warned us against every evil we have in our body politic today. Nothing in this section will be new to anyone who has listened carefully to the general conference addresses over the past few decades. The majority of the American people—and even some of the Saints—have become so accustomed to the transfer of wealth via government that they see it as a "civil right," and they are astonished and angered when anyone suggests that it is wrong. (See also ADC, KKR, and W.)

Take-off Passage

Ether 8:17–26.

Other Passages

1 Nephi 14:1–14; 22:1–23; 2 Nephi 1:6–9; 10:10–21; 26:22; Alma 10:27; 51:5–8; Helaman 1:12; 3:23; 4:22; 5:2; 6:26, 30, 37–40; 7:4–5, 18–21; 8:1–4; 3 Nephi 3:7; 7:6; 10:16; 21:1–4; Ether 2:7–13; 8:19; Doctrine and Covenants 38:11–13, 28–29; 42–64. (See also John Taylor, *Juvenile Instructor,* 22:143 (1881); Jerreld L. Newquist, *Prophets, Principles, and National Survival* [Salt Lake City: Bookcraft, 1964]; Ezra Taft Benson, *An Enemy Hath Done This* [Salt Lake City: Parliament Publishers, 1969]; and J. Reuben Clark, Jr., *Stand Fast by Our Constitution* [Salt Lake City: Deseret Book Co., 1962].)

Study Questions

1. How does the devil work as the leader of all anti-Christian movements?

2. What can you see in the modern political and social scene which seems to follow the philosophy of Gadianton?

3. What ties do you see between the destiny of the Church and the history of America? (See Conference talk by Elder Delbert L. Stapley, October 6, 1963.) What forces are threatening the peace and autonomy of America? If they succeed, what effect will that have on the Church and the missionary system?

4. Why do the enemies of freedom always commence their fight against Christianity and freedom by destroying the right to own and control property? Demonstrate that all true and Constitutional rights are based upon property rights. How does this relate to the Gadianton combinations?

5. Make some historical comparisons between the *modus operandi* of the Gadianton bands (murder, secrecy, robbery, political ambition) and the *modus operandi* of various modern Marxist groups.

The Way of the Sign-Seeker Is to Want Proof Before He Exercises Faith • WSS •

The sign-seeker reasons that, if there were a God and a judgment, God would let him know. He claims he would be the first to live righteously if he only had some reason or evidence. He thinks that if the Book of Mormon is really true, he should be able to see the gold plates or have a revelation before demonstrating his faith. He tells himself these things even if he does not always speak them out loud. He doesn't "speak the truth in his heart." (Psalm 15:2.)

The trouble is that the sign-seeker really loves his sins and does not want to give them up unless he knows he must. He thinks he needs a sign, but what he really needs is a better character. Light is attracted to light and virtue to virtue. (Doctrine and Covenants 88:40.) Jesus implied that there was a preexisting condition in those who rejected him which condemned them. Such "men loved darkness rather than light." (John 3:16–21.) The man of faith is willing to live righteously out of a love for righteousness and a hatred for sins. Signs do not necessarily produce faith, but faith produces signs. However, if signs come we are not to boast about them. And we must not seek signs so that we can "consume them upon our lusts." (Mormon 9:28.)

Take-off Passage

Ether 12:6.

Other Passages

1 Nephi 17:45; Jacob 7:13–20; Alma 30:43–58; 3 Nephi 2:1, 2; 8:4; Moroni 10:22; Matthew 12:39; John 3:18–21; Doctrine and Covenants 84:65–73.

Study Questions

1. How does the story of Laman and Lemuel relate to this subject? Compare their responses to signs with that of Alma the younger.
2. Why don't supernatural manifestations change the hearts of some sinners?
3. Why are signs usually unnecessary?
4. Cite examples from the scriptures which illustrate the thesis of President Spencer W. Kimball's book *Faith Precedes the Miracle.*
5. How are sign-seeking and the spirit of adultery related? (See Matthew 12:38–45.)
6. How do mankind's responsibility and free agency relate to the rules under which signs are given or not given?
7. How does the premortal existence help explain why some enjoy spiritual gifts more readily and easily than others.
8. Why did Jesus teach that the recipient of spiritual manifestations is not guaranteed salvation? (See 3 Nephi 14:22–23.)

Many of the Writers of the Book of Mormon Were Eyewitnesses of Christ • EWC •

This idea of "eyewitnesses" was inspired by that great testimony of Peter: "For we have not followed cunningly devised fables, when we made known unto you the power and coming of our Lord Jesus Christ, but were eyewitnesses of his majesty." (2 Peter 1:16.) Maybe there already were antichrists going about in that day undermining the testimonies of the Apostles. Certainly modern Bible critics have accused Peter and the ancient Church of inventing Jesus's atonement and resurrection after he was gone. In other words, these Bible critics accuse the ancient Saints of introducing the most sacred and basic tenets of Christianity as "cunningly devised fables." But that isn't true. Hundreds saw and felt the resurrected Jesus in Palestine. Thousands saw and felt him in America. And many saw him before and after his personal appearances immediately after his resurrection. They saw him hundreds of years before and hundreds of years after.

It would be hard to find a more appealingly beautiful testimony than that of Moroni given around A.D. 400:

> And now I, Moroni, bid farewell unto the Gentiles, yea, and also unto my brethren whom I love, until we shall meet before the judgment-seat of Christ, where all men shall know that my garments are not spotted with your blood.
>
> And then shall ye know that I have seen Jesus, and that he hath talked with me face to face, and that he told me in plain humility, even as a man telleth another in mine own language, concerning these things;
>
> And only a few have I written, because of my weakness in writing.
>
> And now, I would commend you to seek this Jesus of whom the prophets and apostles have written, that the grace of God the Father, and also the Lord Jesus Christ, and the Holy Ghost, which beareth record of them, may be and abide in you forever. Amen. (Ether 12:38–41.)

Moroni's father, Mormon, was the only writer who gave us more of the Book of Mormon than Moroni. And Mormon, too, said that when he was only fifteen, he was "visited of the Lord, and tasted and knew of the goodness of Jesus." (Mormon 1:15.) This does not necessarily mean that he saw and felt Jesus; but, considering his modesty and considering the many instructions he received regarding the production of the gold plates, it is highly probable that he had reference to something more than the witness of the Spirit.

There is no question that Nephi and Jacob saw Jesus. And there were many others. Such were the great men who wrote the Book of Mormon. They were men to be reckoned with and their words are to be reckoned with.

When the Spirit has come down into your very bones and filled you with that divine and burning testimony of the truth of the Book of Mormon, you will know that Jesus has made himself known in person to many in both ancient and modern times. Joseph, Oliver, and Sidney were not the only modern prophets who saw God. There have been others. Like Mormon, they do not boast and they rarely give the details. But it has ever been thus and will ever be thus. As Jacob said, no one can know much about God except by revelation. (Jacob 4:8.) As long as the works and Church of the Lord are among men, there will be eyewitnesses of Christ so that true and complete faith can flourish.

Take-off Passage

Ether 12:38–40.

Other Passages

1 Nephi 1:9; 2:16; 11:27; 2 Nephi 2:4; 6:9; 11:2, 3; Jacob 7:12; Alma 36:22, 3 Nephi 11:6–15; 17:25; Mormon 1:15; Ether 3:6–16;

12:19, 20; Moroni 7:29–31; Luke 24:48; Acts 10:39–41; 2 Peter 1:16.

Study Questions

1. Alma told Korihor that the testimony of the prophets was a sign to him that God lived. (See Alma 30.) Show how a testimony of the Book of Mormon justifies this assertion.
2. Construct a step-by-step argument to show that a testimony of the truth of the Book of Mormon is proof of the reality and resurrection of Jesus—that he is a God of flesh and bone, an exalted man.
3. Why does the Lord limit the number to whom he actually appears? Why must most of the rest of us get our testimony by starting with the Book of Mormon? Why the Book of Mormon instead of the Bible?
4. Is there any honest, intellectual way that an atheist or an agnostic can disprove the testimony of an eyewitness of Christ?
5. What does this section reveal about the origin and development of religion that is different from the usual approach of worldly scholars?
6. Why were prophets called prophets before the time of Christ? (See 1 Corinthians 14:1 and Revelation 19:10.)

The Power of the Holy Ghost Has Been Available During Every Dispensation • HG •

It is the power of the Holy Ghost which teaches men spiritual things, which testifies of Christ, which tells the prophets of things to come. This power was available to men in ages past and will be in time to come. It must be here now if there are any men or women who are "called" to salvation. That's what Peter said: "For the promise is unto you, and to your children, and to all that are afar off, even as many as the Lord our God shall call." (Acts 2:39.)

What promise is unto even as many as the Lord shall call? The gift of the Holy Ghost. (See verse 38.) To what are they called? To salvation. Hence, if anyone claims to be saved, he must claim the gift of the Holy Ghost. If he claims the gift of the Holy Ghost, he is claiming revelation; for the Holy Ghost does nothing that is not, by definition, revelation, since he is a member of the Godhead. And since revelation is scripture, those churches which claim there can be no scripture besides the Bible are also claiming there can be no one saved since the Bible times. And that is a denial of Peter's promise to his listeners, their children, "and all that are afar off." You see, he knew that in two generations the apostasy would be complete, and then the night of darkness would come and the morning would not break until the gospel would be restored to us who are "afar off."

Under the law of Moses they did not have a legal right to the laying on of hands for the gift of the Holy Ghost. Nevertheless, the Spirit was poured out upon them from time to time. And from Adam to Moses there never was a time when the gift of the Holy Ghost was not available to the Saints of those times.

The Book of Mormon bears witness that if we do not have the Holy Ghost it is because of our own sin and doubt.

Take-off Passage

Moroni 2.

Other Passages

1 Nephi 10:14–22; 11:11; 13:37; 2 Nephi 28:1–6; 31:17, 18; 32:2–5; 33:1, 2; Jacob 7:12–20; Alma 5:44–48; 32:28; 3 Nephi 9:20; Moroni 7:32; 10:4–7; John 14:16, 17, 26; 15:26; 16:7–13; Acts 1:4, 5; 2:37–39; Doctrine and Covenants 8:1–3; 20:43; 68:1–4.

Study Questions

1. What relationships can you see between the power of the Holy Ghost, continual revelation, and one's claim to salvation?
2. How is the Holy Ghost involved in receiving the name of Christ? in becoming a son or daughter of Christ? in entering the strait gate? in being prepared for the final judgment? in getting a testimony of anything, including the Book of Mormon?
3. What reasons and requirements does the Book of Mormon give for manifestations of the Holy Ghost in all ages?
4. How can you use this section in effective missionary work?

The Moral Imperative As Defined by a True Christian Is Christ • MID •

Sincere and knowledgeable totalitarians (state worshipers) of all kinds believe that the supreme good is that which benefits or promotes the goals of the state, and the supreme evil is that which harms or deters the goals of the state. Most humanists (worshipers of humanity), whether knowledgeable or ignorant, believe that right and wrong can and should be determined by a consensus (majority opinion). In other words, the moral imperative of the totalitarians is the state or the goals of the state, and the moral imperative of most humanists is total and unbridled democracy. (Technically, that kind of democracy is also totalitarianism—the tyranny of the majority; but we will ignore that aspect of it.)

Every philosophy or religion has a moral imperative. It is called moral because it involves choices between right and wrong. It is called imperative because it demands attention. It is the standard or criterion which is most important to the adherents of that particular philosophy. It is the standard which will determine how they will vote. It will choose their music, their entertainment, their occupations to a certain extent, their spouses, and will be the basis for every other decision which affects the quality of their lives. Paul told the Roman Saints to avoid those who cause divisions in the Church of God because they do it to "serve . . . their own bellys." (Romans 16:18.) The moral imperative of no end of people is their own belly—at least part of the time. And to have two moral imperatives is to be double-minded. Such a person does not have "an eye single to the glory of God."

The Book of Mormon very clearly tells us the final will and word of God on the method of determining what is good and what is evil. That which persuades us to come to Christ is good and of God, and that which leads away from Christ is evil and of the devil. This is what a true Saint will accept for his or her moral imperative. This truth is one of the best tools for a missionary to use to find the true believers. People who accept this moral imperative will find out that the Book of Mormon is true.

Take-off Passage

Moroni 7:5–22.

Other Passages

2 Nephi 25:28, 29; 32:4–9; 33:2, 5, 10–15; Ether 4:11, 12; Moroni 10:6, 7; Doctrine and Covenants 88:40.

Study Questions

1. How do the concepts given here take the definition of right and wrong out of the realm of personal subjective opinion into the realm of one standard for all men?

2. Why is it untrue that right and wrong are relative and hard to define?

3. Use examples to show how using Christ as your moral imperative can help you make good moral and intellectual decisions or choices.

4. How can you use the above "take-off passage" to show that people are justified in exercising faith in the Book of Mormon, in modern prophets, and in modern revelation? Write your answer to this question as a dialogue with an investigator in which you show him that it is perfectly rational and responsible to believe in these things if he professes a belief in Christ.

God Has Sent Angels from Time to Time to Warn and Bless Us • A •

The word *angel* is a Greek word meaning "messenger." Angels visit men on earth just as surely as airplanes fly from city to city. Some are translated beings and some are resurrected beings. Both of these classes of angels have tangible bodies and can be felt and otherwise discerned by the mortal senses when there is a reason for such a blessing. Still other angels are the "spirits of just men made perfect." These have not yet been resurrected. As spirits they can be discerned only by persons who have been "quickened by the Spirit." This quickening means that those quickened have their spiritual senses and minds released from the bondage of the flesh so that they can see and hear things that ordinary mortals cannot see and hear.

The devil also has "angels" or messengers. These are always spirits of the damned of this earth or of the one-third who were cast out with Lucifer.

Righteous angels come from the presence of God and visit and introduce themselves, usually only to those "of strong faith and a firm mind in every form of godliness." (Moroni 7:30.) "The office of their ministry is to call men unto repentance, and to fulfill and do the work of the covenants of the Father." They "prepare the way among the children of men, by declaring the word of Christ unto the chosen vessels of the Lord." They bear testimony of Jesus as the Christ. (Moroni 7:31.) Their ministry is proof—at least to those to whom they minister—that there is a life after death. Their testimonies will bring men to judgment. (Doctrine and Covenants 20:10–15.)

Take-off Passage

Moroni 7:29–37.

Other Passages

1 Nephi 13:1–5; Mosiah 3:1–3; Alma 10:1–9; 18:30; 3 Nephi 17:24, 25; 28; Luke 1:11–19, 26; Acts 5:19; 12:1–11; Joseph Smith—History 1:30–55; Doctrine and Covenants 20:6–16; 27:5–14; 110:11–16.

Study Questions

1. Who are the ones called the "residue"? Residue from what? What is their blessing? Why do they not ultimately lack anything enjoyed by those visited by angels? (See also D&C 46:13–14.)
2. How could a missionary use the scriptures in this section to help him with Hebrews 13:8 and Revelation 22:18–20?
3. What relationships do you see between this section and WBM and CR?
4. Cite some cases in the Book of Mormon wherein wicked men saw both good and bad angels. How does the devil sometimes appear?

Hope Is a Harbinger of Charity • HC •

There are two hopes—a hope that hopes and a hope that is an assurance of salvation, or the testimony of Jesus. They really are two stages or developments of the same thing. First a man hears of Christ. If he desires to believe (hopes that this story is true), he has the first hope, which leads to faith in Christ. Then, if he exercises this faith in Christ and otherwise lives the commandments, he receives a "hope in Christ," the common Book of Mormon name for a testimony of Jesus. (Cf. D&C 46:13–14.) Then he must maintain a steadfastness of this hope and let it work in him until he develops true charity, which is the "pure love of Christ." This love is the quality of soul which is necessary for happiness in the presence of God. (See also 1 Corinthians 13.)

Take-off Passage

Moroni 7:41.

Other Passages

2 Nephi 31:20; 33:9; Jacob 2:19; 4:4, 6, 11; Alma 5:10; 13:27–30; 27:28; 34:15–17, 40, 41; 58:11; Ether 12:4, 32; Moroni 7:40–48; 9:25; 1 Corinthians 13; Doctrine and Covenants 121:45.

Study Questions

1. Why would it be improbable that a person could develop charity outside the environment of the true Church of Christ?
2. What relationship does the development of charity have to the acceptance of the atonement of Christ?
3. Explain in your own words the difference between a true person of charity and one who simply "goes through the motions" of being a Christian.
4. How has this part of the Book of Mormon added to your understanding of 1 Corinthians 13?
5. Explain how this part of the Book of Mormon could be so similar to 1 Corinthians 13.
6. How can faith lead to hope, and hope lead to faith, and both lead to charity? What faith are we talking about here?

Repentance Is Not Synonymous with Perfection or Reformation • REP •

The Book of Mormon often tells us that we must "repent of all our sins" to be saved. What does that mean? Does it mean that we must be absolutely perfect before we are candidates for salvation? If that were the case, very few of us could have any hope. Does it mean, "If you have truly repented of your sins, you will never do any of them again?" If that were the case, practically no one would have a covenant relationship with Christ. For we all have *some* sins that don't "scoot" the minute we say "scat." And if falling back into some sins from time to time were proof that repentance never occurred in the first place, what would you do with that most encouraging of all scriptures, Mosiah 26:30?

Sometimes saying what a thing is *not* helps to explain what it *is*. For instance, repentance is not the act of moving from imperfection to perfection in one great move. Repentance is a necessary and recurring step on the road to perfection; but it is not perfection itself. Again, repentance is not reformation. A humanist, for example, can reform; but he can't repent without renouncing humanism. One can repent only if he knows about and believes in Christ. And his repentance is not complete unless he has been baptized by immersion for the remission of sins by one holding the true priesthood of God. And a person has not repented if he hasn't experienced a broken heart and a contrite spirit. Reformation is and should be a constant process of improvement and perfection in the lives of all who aspire to greater goodness. But one could spend his life reforming and never repent.

Repentance is an event in which the repentant person, with the help of Christ and the Spirit, turns his life around. He is going one direction (away from God), and he turns around and goes the opposite direction (toward God). It is that time when the carnal man decides to put on Christ and be saved. In the process, he experiences a whole-souled rejection of his past love of sin and decides to devote his life to Christ and to righteousness, as defined by Christ. He feels like the Lamanite king who said, "I will give away all my sins to know thee, and that I may be raised from the dead, and be saved at the last day!" (Alma 22:18.) He comes down in the depths of humility and "considers himself a fool before God." He recognizes the justice of God and the power of Christ and yearns for the salvation which is held out to him through the atonement of Christ.

In a sense, as implied in the scriptures, a person can repent again and again. Yet there is a difference between this first whole-souled turning around that means repentance and the subsequent renewals of steadfastness to the first decision. Enduring to the end means using the principles of faith in Christ and repentance to the end of our mortal lives. That is, whenever we have fallen prey to human weaknesses and strayed from the path, we renew our faith in Christ and our repentance or change of direction.

Also, we should be careful how we teach the "four *R*'s" or "five *R*'s" of repentance. Too many people who use this gimmick fail to relate Christ to it. They are describing something that is more of a humanistic process than a Christian process. It is recognition of Christ which awakens us to repentance. And try as we will—and must—we cannot make a complete restitution for our sins. Much of our "restitution" to our fellowmen is nothing more than an act of contrition—the bringing forth of "fruit meet for repentance." How could you make a complete restitution for adultery, for example? And we cannot even begin to make a restitution to the demands of justice. We could never make a restitution to God that would be sufficient to bring us back into the presence of God without Christ's atonement. He paid the price through his blood. Even if we offered our own blood as a means of restitution, it would be nothing more than an act of contrition—not an act of "blood atonement"; for only Christ's blood atones. We must remember all this when we talk about restitution.

Take-off Passage

Moroni 8:24–26.

Other Passages

Mosiah 3:11, 12; 26:30; Alma 11:34–37; 17:2–4; 22:12–18; 34:30–41; 37:32–34; 39:6; 41:8–10; 42:24; 3 Nephi 18:30–32; 27:19. (The Book of Mormon contains hundreds of passages on repentance.)

Study Questions

1. What does the atonement of Christ give a person who repents?
2. What earthly rewards or incentives are offered to the man who will seek Christ in the spirit of repentance? What heavenly rewards?
3. What messages were delivered by Book of Mormon prophets that caused men to repent? Give examples of how these messages worked.
4. How would a man who knows about Christ approach repentance differently from one who is a deist or a humanist?
5. What is meant by the expression "faith unto repentance"?

Perfection Is a Universal Goal • PER •

The dream of individual and group perfection is universal in the sense that practically all normal people carry it in their minds and hearts. All are utopianists of some sort or another. They think how they would order society if they were all-powerful.

There are basically two kinds of perfectionists: the Christian kind and the humanistic kind.

Christians seek individual perfection first and expect group perfection to come as a by-product of individual perfection. Humanists seek group perfection first and presume that individual perfection will result from the perfection of the organization and environment of the group.

Christians seek to promote perfection by preaching or persuasion. Humanists always enlist the power of government to bring about perfection by force or by "human engineering."

Christians seek to develop a type of internal self-control brought on by conversion to Christ and through Christ. Humanists seek to develop external control by social pressure and fear of governmental reprisal.

Plato's *Republic* was one man's description of how the government ought to engineer perfection. It has been the inspiration behind no end of humanistic utopian dreams during the last several hundred years.

The American Revolution was a true revolution in that it turned its back upon all men's utopias and set up a free society in which each man could pursue his own dreams without interference as long as he himself did not illegally and immorally interfere with others. This revolution created the climate and favorable soil out of which the modern kingdom of God could grow.

The French Revolution was an entirely different affair. The intent of its humanistic backers was to set up utopian liberty, fraternity, and equality, all of them guaranteed by the government. All they got was chaos and violence. And we have seen similar humanistic plans come and go ever since: fascism, Nazism, communism, and Fabian socialism. All of these latter nightmares grew basically out of the dreams of one man, Karl Marx; but he was one in spirit with the French Revolution.

The Book of Mormon reveals the following principles about perfection and utopias:

1. Men cannot establish utopias. Only God can.
2. God establishes utopias in his own time and way by leading off chosen people to chosen places and by destroying the wicked so that the righteous can become perfected in Christ.
3. The only way we can become perfect individually and as a

people is by following Christ, by partaking of his atonement, and by following his laws.

If God creates the climate for utopia and we labor diligently, we can establish Zion. That is the name of God's utopia. The name of the humanistic utopia is Babylon—and it shall fall. After it falls and the earth is cleansed by fire, Zion will be established for a thousand years. That is what we call the Millennium.

Take-off Passage

Moroni 10:32–33.

Other Passages

2 Nephi 31:20; Alma 11:44; 32:34; Moroni 8:16; Matthew 5:48; Doctrine and Covenants 45:46; 50:24; 67:13; 76:69; 107:43; 128:15–18; 129:6.

Study Questions

1. Why is it impossible to perfect mankind by perfecting his environment through social engineering and planning?
2. How does the one-world dream of the gentile nations differ from the doctrines, plans, and destiny of the LDS church? (See Doctrine and Covenants 65.)
3. How does this section (PER) relate to NFM, FA, GW, and NFJ?
4. What teachings of the Book of Mormon would your children have to understand and accept to lay a foundation for perfection?

Appendix: Sample Marked Page

righteousness nor happiness there
be no punishment nor misery.
And if these things are not there
is no God. And if there is no
God we are not, neither the earth;
for there could have been no creation of things, neither to act nor
to be acted upon; wherefore, all
things must have vanished away.
14. And now, my sons, I speak
unto you these things for your
profit and learning; for there is
a God, and he hath created all
things, both the heavens and the
earth, and all things that in them
are, both things to act and things
to be acted upon.
15. And to bring about his
eternal purposes in the end of
man, after he had created our
first parents, and the beasts of
the field and the fowls of the air,
and in fine, all things which are
created, it must needs be that
there was an [h]opposition; even
the forbidden fruit in opposition
to the tree of life; the one being
sweet and the other bitter.
16. Wherefore, the Lord God
gave unto man that he should
act for himself. Wherefore, man
could not act for himself save it
should be that he was enticed by
the one or the other.
17. And I, Lehi, according to
the things which I have read,
must needs suppose that an angel
of God, according to that [i]which
is written, had fallen from heav-
en; wherefore, he became a devil,
having sought that which was evil
before God.
18. And because he had fallen
from heaven, and had become
miserable forever, he sought also
the misery of all mankind. Wherefore, he said unto Eve, yea, even
that old serpent, who is the devil,
who is the father of all lies,
wherefore he said: Partake of
the forbidden fruit, and ye shall
not die, but ye shall be as God,
knowing good and evil.
19. And after Adam and Eve
had partaken of the forbidden
fruit they were driven out of
the garden of Eden, to till the
earth.
20. And they have brought
forth children; yea, even the
family of all the earth.
21. And the days of the children of men were prolonged, according to the will of God, that
they might repent while in the
flesh; wherefore, their state became a state of probation, and
their time was lengthened, according to the commandments
which the Lord God gave unto
the children of men. For he gave
commandment that all men must
repent; for he showed unto all
men that they were lost, because
of the transgression of their
parents.
22. And now, behold, if Adam
had not transgressed he would
not have fallen, but he would
have remained in the garden of
Eden. And all things which
were created must have remained
in the same state in which they
were after they were created; and
they must have remained forever, and had no end.
23. And they would have had
[j]no children; wherefore they
would have remained in a state
of innocence, having no joy, for
they knew no misery; doing no
good, for they knew no sin.
24. But behold, all things have
been done in the wisdom of him
who knoweth all things.
25. Adam [k]fell that men might

h, ver. 11. *i*, ver. 18. 2 Ne. 9:8. Mos. 16:3. P. of G. P., Moses 4:3—4. Abraham 3:27, 28. Gen. 3:1. Rev. 12:9. 20:2. *j*, ver. 25. P. of G. P., Moses 5:11. *k*, ver. 23. BETWEEN B. C. 588 AND 570.

PD 2Ne 2:27-29 2Ne 9:8,9; 2Ne 28 especially v. 21-22
Mos 2:32-39, Al 5:39-42, Al 30:53 Al 37:33 Hel 14:30-31 3Ne 18:18

FA 2Ne 9:6; Mos 3:19 Mos 16:3-8
Al 12:21-27 Al 42:2-7 Hel 14:16
Morm 9:12-13 Eth 3:2 Moses 4:6-32
Moses 5:4-11

Index to Coded Subjects

About the Authors

Born in Ririe, Idaho, and raised in West Jordan, Utah, Glenn Pearson served in an airborne unit in World War II. He obtained his B.S. in History from Utah State University and his M.A. in Bible and Modern Scripture from Brigham Young University, and he has completed his course work for a doctorate. He has served as a full-time missionary, stake mission president, bishop, high councilor, member of the general Church Missionary Preparation Committee, and temple officiator. A teacher and writer by profession, he taught at BYU for 22 years, has been director of the UCLA and Santa Monica City College LDS Institutes of Religion, and has written manuals for Church college curriculum. He is married to the former Ardith Hunsaker and the couple have five children.

Reid Bankhead was born in Logan, Utah, served as a naval officer in World War II, and obtained his B.S. in Civil Engineering from the University of Utah and his M. Th. from BYU, where he has taught for over thirty-six years. In addition to his two-year mission, his Church callings have included various teaching assignments (including teaching weekly in the Salt Lake City Mission Home for twelve years), bishop's counselor, stake missionary, bishop, mission president, and high councilor. He and his wife, the former Mary Smith, have eight children.